# Joseph Smith
## *the Prophet*

T. Gorka 1989

# Joseph Smith
## the Prophet

## TRUMAN G. MADSEN

BOOKCRAFT
Salt Lake City, Utah

Frontispiece illustration
*"This Is My Prophet of the Last Dispensation"*
by Ted Gorka

**Library of Congress Catalog Card Number 89-62192**

ISBN 0-88494-704-1

Printed in the United States of America          72076-0217R

20   19   18   17   16   15   14   13

# Contents

# Introduction

Here is the printed version of the "Joseph Smith tapes."

More than all else I have written or recorded, these cassettes have engendered a return wave, international in scope, of responsive letters and comments. Apparently we live in a new era of catch-all listening: the padded earphones of the "Walkman," the car-cassette playback, the ever-faster computer access to ever-larger "databases."

Recurrent questions include these: Where were the lectures given? To whom was I talking? Why was the material recorded instead of written? Whence my long-standing interest in Joseph Smith? How is it that I talk as if I know him? How reliable are the many documents I cite, and where can they be found? Where might one go to read more? The most frequent query has been, "When are you going to publish the lectures and provide the sources?"

The lectures were delivered at Brigham Young University's Marriott Center during an Education Week. That a goodly number came to give eight hours of undivided—or even divided—attention to these two-a-day classes was a manifestation of the richness of the subject. The audience was "in-house." With them I could begin with presumptions and assurances which to others would have appeared startling. But between the lines I was also thinking of many who had posed penetrating queries about Joseph Smith over the years, both in and out of the classroom. They were an "invisible" audience. And at certain points it is apparent that I was addressing them, in a kind of underground conversation, more than those present.

My motive in tape recording rather than writing was to press through the written sources to the center of the man. Elsewhere, and in a technical way, I have written much about the teachings of Joseph Smith (see bibliography). Here the attempt was to present the teacher. The more I have worked with the Joseph Smith materials, the more I have sensed dimensions, perceptions, levels of awareness, the sounding of chords, nuances, that defy full expression. They are matters of the spirit and the heart. In the jargon of our time, they tie to the "depth-self." They are the truth that waits beyond the skeletal facts. In this realm no one can fully communicate. But one can often come closer in the spoken than in the written mode.

On this point Joseph Smith's renewing influence was almost unique. In the three major monotheistic religions—Judaism, Christianity, and Islam—there is a long-standing respect for written texts; sometimes, strange to say, a veneration so intense that it excludes God, as if the written word itself were identical with God. Joseph Smith reopened the canon. He insisted on the vitality and cruciality of the new and living word as well as of the old. But he went further. For him, comprehensive religious understanding occurs only at the speaking of a living voice attended by the living Spirit of God. This is the "sealing up of the law and the binding up of the testimony." Therefore, in the final reckoning, none of us, he taught, would be enlightened or condemned on "dead testimony" alone. In that spirit I chose to speak rather than write. For like reasons I have, until now, resisted requests that I put the lectures in print.

Is this book's set of approaches exhaustive? Hardly. It is just one more beginning. Neither in this nor in other essays have I felt equal to the vastness of the relevant materials or to the full range of the Prophet's teaching. In my judgment nothing so far published —whether biographical, historical, or expository—is fully adequate. With due respect to my colleagues who have made attempts in these categories—and they deserve far more respect than they have so far received—we still await a "definitive" work. Since, as I believe, no one person can completely master the immediate and world context into which Joseph Smith came, and the texts that survive him, we may never see a one-author definitive work. In the meantime, probing the earliest sources in such topical fashion, segmented and piecemeal though it be, is the order of the day.

How reliable are the documents? Professional historians will continue hard analysis of the materials to see the man as he really was. Extremists will insist nothing can be known. Other extremists will suppose they have arrived at the final portrait. With respect to the documents I try to be a patient, winnowing scientist. In evaluation I try to be, in the most inclusive sense, subjective. For those who are sure that the cause of truth is not served by such a combination it will be best to change the subject. In these lectures I do not change the subject. The subject is Joseph Smith as Prophet. I have tried to read all who claimed to know him. Here I am outlining, fleshing, and comparing all at once.

Many letters have asked whether I do not overstate the significance of the man. In one sense I believe he himself would say I do. He has a place. But not the only place. One of the recurrent messages of his life was that every generation needs its righteous men and women, and that for the contemporary audience the living leader takes precedence over those who are dead and gone.

But in another sense it is hard to overstate his significance. Using the measuring rod of present growth rates, by the last quarter of the twenty-first century there will be 260,000,000 Latter-day Saints. Thus, say the statisticians, will emerge the "first world religion" since the rise of Islam, a redefinition of the Jewish-Christian tradition reaching into all lands and cultures. If this, or anything like it, turns out to be so, then there will be increasing interest in the seminal figure of this modern era and in the origin-events of the Restoration. It has always been difficult to ignore

Joseph Smith. Soon enough, if the demographers are right, it will be impossible.

"I calculate," he said less than two months before his death, "to be one of the instruments of setting up the kingdom of Daniel by the word of the Lord, and I intend to lay a foundation that will revolutionize the whole world."[1] Latter-day Saints accept the pronouncement that came through his successor: "Which foundation he did lay, and was faithful."[2] The staggering boldness of the man is a constant amazement to me—more, not less, as I work in the areas of comparative religion and look for his like in the long train of prophets, savants, and patriarchs.

It must also be said of Joseph Smith that he has no stature at all except in his ties with the Master. Much modern scholarship deals with the window frame and the window rather than the vista. Many have claimed to see through Joseph Smith; I am among the number. But it still makes good copy and conversation to speak of him as puzzling, mysterious, enigmatic, inexplicable. Many books and articles flourish on that premise. For the things that matter most, however—and what mattered most to him and those who surrounded him was the way of the prophets and ultimately the way of Christ—he is not only clear; he is transparent. It is fascinating enough to study the window; I myself have not resisted the temptation. But that is not what I am dwelling on here. I am dwelling on what one may see *through* the window. In doing so I am making a call to what is vital.

The tape format enabled me to be conversational, intimate, and also to relate to my listeners on personal implications, preoccupied at each stage with the questions, "What does all this have to do with me?" Something of that style remains in this book. Some corrections made in the written manuscript have been factual. Most are cosmetic: for grammar, for clarity. In the lectures I often paraphrased and approximated. Here, in either the text or the notes the quotations are given precisely, sometimes with alternative versions and sometimes also with a word or two about the setting and the date. During the lectures I often said, "You know" and "As you remember," in familiar mode. Here these phrases often have been removed.

As for my notes and sources, they point to a veritable feast of documents. They are designed to continue the conversation. For each of the points I make there is often more, and perhaps better, documentation and amplification of the story. Two things should be apparent in the notes: (1) my preoccupation with firsthandedness, and even for late recollections if they claim to be firsthanded; (2) a preference for those who had the longest and most multifaceted relationships with the Prophet.

That leads to the question of title. It is simply, "Joseph Smith the Prophet." But it might well have been titled "Joseph Smith for Our Times." That is because he is both with us and ahead of us. He is not boxed up in the nineteenth century. He was, and is, really ahead of his time. He and those around him wrote a modern book of Acts. They wrote it both in aspiration and in experience. It was transmitted by men and women who were eye-witnesses, who shared "the heat and the burden of the day." The book is unfinished, not because the author disappeared but because new chapters are being written every day.

There have always been movements that, to get more light out of the scriptures, have come at them from different angles, trying to "do it with mirrors." If that enterprise were not partly justified, scholars would be among the unemployed and the unemployable. But for Joseph Smith the triumphant way to God is through a channel of light: direct, visionary, and discernible; such light as was manifest on the ascent to Sinai, on the road to Damascus, or in the Sacred Grove.

Of the letters that mean most to me, one ended, "It was the first time I took Joseph Smith seriously." The letter described how the writer and his wife—who as I write this are in Hong Kong—went from a fragmented and secular life to a Christ-centered life. If my elementary sifting of documents and sharing of impressions moves others to look not simply at Joseph Smith but through him to the Master—and, with those insights, to take a searching look at themselves—my efforts will have been more than worthwhile.

# The First Vision and Its Aftermath

Years ago I prepared a paper titled "Joseph Smith Among the Prophets."[1] It attempted to present ten characterizations of prophets that are typical in Judeo-Christian literature. For instance, a prophet is a foreteller; he has prophetic access to the future. Also, prophets have been called "forth-tellers," meaning that they speak forth boldly in judgment and in recommendation as to their own time. A prophet too is a man who has authority, who speaks with more than human sanction. He is a recoverer or discoverer of truth. He is an advocate of social righteousness. He is a charismatic, one whose personality manifests something that attracts in a spiritual sense. He is one who endures suffering, and does so radiantly. He is an embodiment of love. He is a seer, meaning that he has the capacity to clearly understand and reveal truth. Finally, among the great prophets of the past, many have been martyrs.

In that presentation I showed that, under each of those heads, Joseph Smith qualifies as a prophet. If we can use any one of them to characterize a prophet, what can we say of a man who manifests them all?

In this chapter, more intimately than in the Judeo-Christian captions above, we come to a subjective approach to Joseph's glorious first vision.

In 1969 *BYU Studies* published a collection of the four known written accounts of the First Vision.[2] One was first recorded in 1832; another in 1835, after a visit Joseph had with a Jewish visitor named Matthias; there is the 1838 statement, which has been published to the world in the Pearl of Great Price; and finally, the well-known Wentworth letter written in 1842 to the *Chicago Democrat*, in which the Prophet briefly recapitulated his first vision. What was intended by the *BYU Studies* publication was not only to give, as was done, the actual holographs—the handwritten accounts from his different scribes—as he dictated them, but also to provide articles on the context by some of the best LDS scholars.[3]

In the earliest account, Joseph speaks of his days in Vermont. There and later in New York Joseph would look up at night and marvel at the symmetry and the beauty and the order of the heavens. Something in him said, "Behind that there must be a majestic creator of the heavens."[4] The contrast between his boyhood awareness and the confusion he saw on this planet was not just difficult; it seared his soul.[5] The divisions he laments in Palmyra were not just among and between others, neighbors and friends; they were in his own family. He had at least one relative in every church in Palmyra, so that his family was utterly spread. Order in heaven, disorder on earth. How could God be responsible for both?

The record makes it clear that before the sacred experience in the Grove it had never occurred to Joseph that all the influential churches were in error. The question he put to Jesus Christ when he recovered himself was not, "Is there a true church in the world?" The question was, "Which church is true?" He assumed that at least one had to be true. The answer therefore was all the more striking and startling: "Join none of them."[6]

By reading in the Bible Joseph had been "struck"—in fact he says, "Never did any passage of scripture come with more power to the heart of man than this did at this time to mine."[7] The Reverend George Lane may have been the man who first recommended in Joseph Smith's hearing, "Let him ask of God." That specific passage in James 1:5 was mentioned in some of the minister's sermons. A Methodist, he was associated with revivals in western New York.[8] Joseph later talks of a Methodist preacher he was with soon after the vision, a person who was, he says, "active in the before mentioned religious excitement." Imagine (and this to me is poignant) Joseph at age fourteen—full as he was of the glory, the remarkable experience and the excitement of it—recounting his experience to this man. And the man's response was, "Oh no, that could not be of God. Those things don't happen anymore."

So one lacking wisdom ought to go and pray about it. By all means let him ask of God. But to this man the answer seemed . . . well, too much. Heaven had come too close. We can almost visualize the boy—pure-minded, spontaneous, even a little unrestrained as teenagers are—being struck by the wonder of this marvelous answer to prayer. "Wow! It worked! You told me to do it. I did it." And the response was, "Shucks, boy, it's all of the devil."[9] The boy's smile slowly disappeared. And he learned early that to testify of divine manifestations was to stir up darkness and to call down wrath. That wrath finally evolved into bullets.

The enemies of Joseph Smith have made out over and over that he was shiftless, lazy, indolent, that he never did a day's work in his life.[10] But a document exists that contains reported recollections about Joseph Smith as recorded by Martha Cox. One of these comes from a woman, identified as Mrs. Palmer, who knew him in his early life when she was a child.[11] As a girl—years younger than him, apparently—she watched him with others of the boys working on her father's farm. Far from his being indolent, the truth is that, according to this account, her father hired Joseph because he was such a good worker.[12]

Another reason was that Joseph was able to get the other boys to work. The suspicion is that he did that by the deft use of his fists. It is my belief that one of the feelings he had of unworthiness, one of the things for which he asked forgiveness (and his account shows that he did pray for forgiveness prior to the visitations of Moroni), was this physical propensity. He was so strong, so muscular, so physically able, that that was one way he had of solving problems. This troubled him. He did not feel it was consonant with the divine commission he had received.[13]

Mrs. Palmer's account speaks of "the excitement stirred up among some of the people over [Joseph's] first vision." A churchman, she recalls, came to her father "to remonstrate against his allowing such close friendship between his family" and the boy Joseph. But the father, pleased with Joseph's work on his farm, was determined to keep him on. Of the vision, he said that it was "the sweet dream of a pure-minded boy." Later, the daughter reports, Joseph claimed to have had another vision; and this time it led to the production of a book. The churchman came again, and at this point the girl's father turned against Joseph. But, she adds significantly, by then it was too late. Joseph Smith had a following.[14]

The first members of that following were his family, who supported and loved him with great constancy. In fact there is no greater example of total familial endurance in history than that of the Smith family. It is true that they had their ups and downs and that William Smith was almost as insecure and unsteady as Hyrum Smith was loyal and unyielding. But from an overall perspective, one of the strengths of the history of the Church is that the first family held true to each other.[15] Even in the early days of Joseph's revelations, the father would counsel him not to be disobedient to the heavenly vision.[16]

The 1838 account of the First Vision describes the struggle Joseph had with the adversary. At crucial turning points in the Restoration, Beelzebub, the enemy of righteousness, the prince of darkness, has made his power felt.[17] The First Vision was a natural point of attack. The devil has not, like the rest of us, lost his memory of premortal life. He has not been placed in a physical body and had the veil drawn. He therefore knew Joseph Smith. Later in his life Joseph would say, "Every man [and that would include himself] who has a calling to minister to the inhabitants of the world was ordained to that very purpose in the Grand Council of heaven before this world was."[18] It is no surprise, then, that the adversary would wish to thwart the earnest supplications of the boy Joseph in the Sacred Grove. It was not the first time someone had prayed for the Lord to answer the hard question, "Where is the truth?" The response that came to Joseph was an answer, I believe, to millions of prayers offered down through the centuries on both sides of the veil.

How strong was the dark influence on that occasion? In the Pearl of Great Price account Joseph makes clear that it was no imaginary thing. For a time it seemed as if he would be destroyed.[19] In an earlier account he adds that for a time he could not speak, as if his tongue cleaved to the roof of his mouth.[20] He exerted faith and was released from the evil power.

Throughout his life the Prophet had important things to say about the power of the evil one, but he never said the evil one was as powerful as the living God. He knew both. Like Moses of old,[21] he was not confused when once he had experienced both and felt their influence. Speaking of the kind of power that we call possession, he taught the Saints that "the devil has no power over us only as we permit him."[22] He said elsewhere that all men have power to resist the devil. All, in short, is voluntary.[23] But whether we are righteous or not, we do not escape the attacks. And they can come from the outside, as in Joseph's case in the Grove or, if we yield, they can become interior and we ourselves can become the very puppets of the evil one. A healthy respect, if I may put it so, for the power of darkness arose from Joseph Smith's early vision, as did a glorious respect for the power that overcomes darkness.[24]

Joseph described the descending light. In dictating the account, he sought the proper word. He first used the word *fire*. That is crossed out in favor of *spirit* or *light*. The word he finally settled on and used most often was *glory*. It refers to the emanating and radiating spirit and power of God.[25] But the word *fire* is important to notice. Orson Pratt, in his book *Interesting Account of Several Remarkable Visions*—published in 1840, two years before the Wentworth letter, and circulated widely in the missions in Great Britain and Europe—says that the young prophet expected to see "the leaves and boughs of the trees consumed."[26] In other words, he thought he was seeing descending fire, the kind that burns and consumes. Was that detail something Orson Pratt had learned from conversation with the Prophet? Or was it an inference from the statement Joseph makes that the "brightness and glory defy all description"? The Prophet indicates in the 1835 account that he was filled with that light, but also surrounded by it, that it filled the Grove. Then he adds, "yet nothing consumed," perhaps indicating that he expected it to be.[27]

The Prophet was not harmed by the experience; he was hallowed by it. Having seen the light, he now saw in it two personages, one of whom said to him, indicating the other, "This is my Beloved Son." In the Wentworth letter the Prophet adds, speaking of the two, that they "exactly resembled each other in features, and likeness."[28] Notice they not just resembled—they *exactly* resembled each other in features and likeness. We speak of a family resemblance: "Like father, like son." The Son looked like his Father. Philip asked, "Show us the Father." The Master replied, "Have I been so long time with you, and yet hast thou not known me, Philip? He that hath seen me hath seen the Father."[29] This is not because they are identical but because they are, in appearance as well as in nature, exactly similar.

This circumstance may give further insight into the phrase Alma used in his familiar set of questions about our spiritual progress: "Is the image of God engraven upon your countenances?"[30] It may also give greater meaning to a favorite story of President David O. McKay's about the great stone face: in the very loving of a countenance one may eventually take on the character of what one loves.[31] It gives further confirmation of the Prophet's later vision of the Twelve while in Kirtland—a disparate group of men from a variety of backgrounds whom he saw in vision, through their flounderings and struggles, until he saw them glorified. He saw them welcomed by father Adam, ushered to the throne of God, greeted and embraced by the Master, and then crowned. "He saw that they all had beautiful heads of hair and *all looked alike*."[32] This should not be pushed to mean that the Twelve had absolutely similar features, but rather that in glory, "in bloom and beauty"—and the Prophet uses the word *beauty* to describe the glory of a resurrected man as well as of a woman—they were similar.[33]

Young Joseph Smith learned in the Sacred Grove that to see the Father is to see the Son, and vice versa.

A deeper point is the relationship of these two beings. Joseph taught in the 1840s—and I think it was an extension of what he learned in the Grove that morning—that the statement of the Master about his doing nothing but what he had seen the Father do has infinite implications.[34] How could Jesus have seen the acts of the Father as a witness? President Joseph Fielding Smith wrote: "The statement of our Lord that he could do nothing but what he had seen the Father do, means simply that it had been revealed to him what his Father had done. Without doubt, Jesus came into the world subject to the same condition as was required of each of us —he forgot everything, and he had to grow from grace to grace."[35]

Again, the relationship is exact. If Christ himself was uniquely begotten and was the firstborn in the spirit, and if he was the Christ not only of this earth but also, as the Prophet taught later, of the galaxy, so before him the Father himself was a Redeemer, having worked out the salvation of souls of whom he was a brother, not a father. This is deep water. The conclusion is drawn by Joseph Smith in his King Follett discourse.[36] Whatever else it may mean, and it is mind-boggling, it at least means this: The Father, by experience, knows exactly what his Son has been through. And the Son, by experience, knows exactly what the Father has been through. Therefore, when he says "I and my Father are one," he is not expressing a metaphysical identity. He is speaking of oneness of spirit, harmonic throbbings of love and insight that can come only in the patterns of eternal redemption. Sown in the mind of a fourteen-year-old boy, that seed of insight blossomed and grew.

Though we do not know how long the Prophet Joseph was in the Grove that day receiving instructions, it probably was longer than is suggested by the outline we have. We know, for example, that he wrote, "Many other things did he say unto me, which I cannot write at this time."[37] So far as I know, he never did commit them to paper. Some critics have pointed out that the Prophet spoke of the visit of angels in connection with his first vision. Some have theorized that he began by asserting that he saw an angel and ended by embellishing it with the claim that he saw the Father and the Son. The truth is that, having described all that we are familiar with about the visitation of the Father and the Son, he says in the closing words of the 1835 account, "I saw many angels in this vision."[38] It is an enforced either-or to say that he either saw the Father and the Son or saw angels. What he saw was both.

Who would have been permitted to be with him in that theophany—what angels were present? This is an unanswerable question. We have Joseph Smith's teaching that angels are either (1), resurrected personages who have lived upon this earth, or (2), the spirits of the just who have lived here and will yet be resurrected, or (3), as in the rare cases in the Old Testament, not-yet-embodied persons who come in anticipation. "There are no angels who minister to this earth but those who do belong or have belonged to it."[39]

Joseph was wearied with his experience in the Grove. The encounter, however long or short, demanded much from him. He says, "I came to myself."[40] I think it inappropriate to say that he had been in a trance or a mystic state. The clearest parallels come from the ancient records of Moses and Abraham and Enoch. Like those prophets of old, Joseph was filled with a spirit which enabled him to endure the presence of God.[41] Is that spirit enervating or is it energizing? My considered answer is, "Yes." It is both. It demands from us a concentration and a surrender comparable to nothing else possible in this life. But it also confers great capacities that transcend our finite mental, spiritual, and physical powers.

In 1832, emerging from the vision on the three degrees of glory (Doctrine and Covenants 76) with his companion in the vision, Sidney Rigdon, the Prophet looked strong, while Sidney was limp and pale. To this the Prophet, with a certain humility as also perhaps with a little condescension, said, "Sidney is not as used to it as I am."[42] But after the First Vision, he was feeble. It was difficult for him to go home. Similarly, in his 1823 encounter with Moroni, the repetitive encounter, he was left weak, and his father sent him home. He couldn't even climb the fence, though he was usually a strong and vigorous boy. Neibaur reports him saying of his condition immediately following the First Vision, "I . . . felt uncommon feeble."[43]

We now turn to some of the theological extensions of this initial insight of the First Vision as the Prophet later taught them. "It is the first principle of the gospel," he said, "to know for a certainty

the character of God." That is more than saying it is the first principle to know *that* God exists. He doesn't use the word *existence* at
all in this context. You can't find one argument in Joseph Smith
for the existence of God. Why not? One answer: Because one does
not begin to argue about a thing's existence until serious doubts
have arisen. The arguments for God are a kind of whistling in the
dark. In the absence of experience with God, men have invented
arguments to justify the experience of the absence of God. They
have built a rational Tower of Babel, from which they comfort
themselves with, "We haven't heard from God, but he must still be
there."

But Joseph wasn't speculating. He was reporting his firsthand
experience. Prophets always have. On the other hand, the philosophers have expended some of the greatest ingenuity of the western
world in inventing what turn out to be specious and invalid arguments for the existence of God. No. "It is the first principle of the
gospel to know for a certainty the character [the personality, the
attributes] of God, and to know that we may converse with him as
one man converses with another."[44] That is the testimony of
Joseph Smith from beginning to end. He is talking about all of us,
now. A man, a woman—it is the first principle for any of us. That
is where we begin.

And lest we should say, as occasionally we do, "But his remarkable life and experience is utterly beyond my own," we
should note that Joseph said in 1839: "God hath not revealed anything to Joseph [calling himself by name], but what He will make
known unto the Twelve, and even the least Saint may know all
things as fast as he is able to bear them." Even the least Saint, I repeat. The Prophet continued: "For the day must come when no
man need say to his neighbor, Know ye the Lord; for all shall
know Him (who remain) from the least to the greatest."[45] Note
that "all shall know him" is different from knowing *about* him.

That same year Joseph delivered a marvelous discourse in
which he expounded on the fourteenth chapter of John, that masterful sermon of the Savior's in which he said that he and the
Father would "make their abode" with faithful Saints. In this address the Prophet in effect readdresses that sermon to us. It is as if
he said, "It is not enough for you to say, 'Ah, Brother Joseph is in

charge, and he knows.' You must know." He says it in ten different ways. Then in the final part he says, "Come to God." These blessings are intended for his Saints, so ask him.[46]

"Well," one might feel, "I don't want to overdo it. I don't want to ask for things I shouldn't ask for." Of course, as a general principle that represents a genuine, discerning wisdom—we should not ask for what we should not seek from him. But when the Lord has commanded us to ask, it is appropriate. This is illustrated in the Savior's parable of the unjust judge and the importunate widow, which is preceded by the reason it was given—to show "that men ought always to pray, and not to faint." It told of the widow who repeatedly came to the judge to plead her case. Always he refused to heed. But because she came back so often, in order to be permanently rid of her the judge said, "All right! Give her what she wants and end her clamoring."[47]

My rendering is a crude paraphrase of the parable. But what is the point of the story? Why would the Savior teach a parable like that? The point is, pray and don't faint; or, in the words of Joseph Smith, "Weary [the Lord] until he blesses you."[48] There are places in modern scripture where the Lord commands someone not to pray further on a particular matter, where he says, "Trouble me no more." But in each case the context shows he had already given the answer, and he is saying, "Please take no or yes for an answer."[49]

So it is. We have the privilege to recapitulate the experience of the Prophet.

That leads to my final point. So often we are haunted not only with the question whether we have gone far enough in our own religious experience but also whether we can rely on some things we have previously trusted. Acids eat away at us. Sometimes it is the taunting of other voices; but sometimes it is nothing more profound than our own sins and weaknesses, and the betrayals of the best in ourselves. Doubt naturally follows.

The Master made a strange statement to Thomas. Thomas is categorized as a doubter because he said what the others had said earlier: "I will believe when, and only when, I see."[50] According to Luke, the others virtually rubbed their eyes in disbelief when they did see. It is a beautiful phrase: "They yet believed not for joy."[51]

Meaning what? Meaning it was too good to be true. Within days they had seen their Lord crucified, and now he stood before them! So they too had impending doubts, as did Thomas. The strange words of Jesus are reported by John: "Thomas, because thou hast seen me, thou hast believed: blessed are they that have not seen, and yet have believed."[52]

On the surface this statement seems to put a premium on secondhand or distant awareness, almost as if unsupportable faith is more commendable than faith resting on the knowledge of sight. That, I think, is a mistake. What is involved in the statement is the recognition by the Lord and by his prophets that the most penetrating of assurances—the one power, even beyond sight, that can burn doubt out of us and make it, as it were, impossible for us to disbelieve—is the Holy Ghost.[53]

Recording the feelings he had on leaving the Grove and on the subsequent days, Joseph left on record this sentence: "My soul was filled with love and for many days I could rejoice with great joy and the Lord was with me but [I] could find none that would believe the heavenly vision."[54] This is one of the rare insights he gives as to what went on inside as distinct from outside him in that experience. Joy, love. And no doubt. Others, of course, doubted. He did not.

The devil is shrewd with the stratagems and with the Satanic substitute, but one thing he cannot counterfeit is the witness and power of the Holy Ghost. When that is upon us there is assurance —and, I repeat, even greater than that of sight. It is of course possible to have both, and that is precisely what Joseph Smith had. He saw, as a later revelation explains, not through the natural or the carnal mind[55] but with the spiritual. He saw with his own eyes, but he also was enveloped in that radiating power which has been commissioned to bear witness of the Father and the Son. Without having open or remarkable visions, we all can have the same glorious and glorifying certainty about the reality of the Father and the Son; and that comes by the Spirit, by the power of the Holy Ghost.

Often we are confronted in the world by those who want to believe in God without believing in God.[56] They are willing to affirm that there is something—and that's about the strongest word they are willing to use—that there is something out there that accounts for things: a principle, a harmonic force, or an ultimate cosmic mystery. How rarely is the testimony welcomed that the Father is in the likeness of the Christ! One reason—and Latter-day Saints can testify of this—is that such personal beings can get involved in your life, changing it, giving specific commandments and counsels, rebuking, approving, or disapproving. A God who is utterly distant stays out of your hair.[57]

It is unlikely that the Prophet fully anticipated the consequences of his prayer in the Grove, but he nevertheless fully measured up to those consequences. He never wavered. On one occasion he said, "If I had not actually got into this work and been called of God, I would back out." But he added—and this shows his integrity—"I cannot back out: I have no doubt of the truth."[58] (Some men having no doubt of the truth have nevertheless backed out, but he did not.) From the Grove experience on throughout his life he knew and welcomed into his life the Father and the Son, "even," as he was commanded in 1829, "if [he] should be slain."[59] He was true unto life and unto death. To use the word that he re-revealed in our generation, that seals the power of his first and subsequent visitations. Anyone who has enough of the Spirit of God to know that God lives and that Jesus is the Christ, by that same spirit will be brought to recognize that one of the prophets called by the Father and the Son was Joseph Smith.

# Joseph's Personality and Character

Let us now do a close-up of the personality and character of the Prophet Joseph Smith.

May I begin with the comment of the late Sidney B. Sperry, who was perhaps the Church's most knowledgeable Hebraist. He studied years ago with some of the world's renowned scholars at the University of Chicago and then came to Brigham Young University, where he remained for his entire career. One reason he studied ancient languages was to gain the advantage of reading in the earlier source materials. Because of his scholarly achievements, some of his colleagues spoke of him as "the accomplished SBS."[1] Early in his life, he said, he had aspired to know more about the scriptures than any man living. He told me, and this is the point, that he had become aware that no man in this generation could possibly know as much about the scriptures as did the Prophet Joseph Smith.

I begin with that because a feeling constantly recurs as one studies the life of Joseph Smith. You never quite get to the bottom. There is always more. You can be so impressed and overcome with glimpses that you say, "Nothing good that I could learn of him would be surprising." And then you become surprised. There is always more. It takes deep to comprehend deep, and I often wonder if any of us have the depth to fully comprehend this man.[2]

In this chapter I want to focus not so much on his prophetic character and gifts as on the characteristics observed by those who surrounded him—on Joseph Smith the man.

Consider for a moment his appearance. We know from the record that he was, in his prime, a little over six feet in height. He weighed over two hundred pounds.[3] One of his advantages all through life was an extremely vigorous and dynamic physical constitution. Without that, he might not have survived the first major crisis of his life—at seven or eight years of age a bone infection, which in most instances required amputation. The doctor, under the pleading of Mother Smith, finally consented to perform less drastic surgery, of course without anesthetic. If you can imagine a section of your leg bone being bored into then broken off in pieces with forceps while you are fully conscious, you will understand what the boy endured. Doctor Wirthlin, in our generation, has shown that one physician from Dartmouth Medical College in New Hampshire was the only man in the United States who understood how to perform that operation and who had the compassion and the skill to do so.[4] That's only one glimpse of Joseph's hardy, enduring physical constitution. Even at that, he bore all he could bear and was prematurely old at age thirty-eight.[5]

The death mask applied by George Cannon, a convert from England, to the face of Joseph (as also one to Hyrum) after the Carthage assassination gives us the exact lineaments of the Prophet's forehead, his hairline, which was in 1844 receding some, partly as a result of poisoning.[6] His nose was, as the statue on Salt Lake City's Temple Square depicts, unusually large. And yet it is the comment of those visiting from the East and of his own convert friends that he was a magnificent man. The word *handsome* recurs, and there are references, at least in the earlier years, to the color and abundance of his hair. It was an auburn cast.[7] There was something of a transparency about his countenance. He was beardless: he shaved, but he did not have a heavy or thick beard. Of the shape of his body, one writer says that there was "no breakage" about it. He had a strong and robust pair of shoulders and from there tapered down.[8] He had become a little portly in the late years at Nauvoo.

There were few manly sports that he didn't have a try at, and many in which he excelled. For example, he wrestled, and wrestled effectively.[9] He jumped at the mark. In this activity you simply drew a mark on the ground, then jumped and marked where you landed, then challenged someone else to match or exceed the jump.[10] He pulled up stakes: Here two men faced each other, placing feet against feet, and then pulled; the stronger one remained on the ground, the other came up. There's another version of that in which, face to face, you hold a pole, like a broomstick, and then pull down. The stronger of the two holds, and his hands don't slip. The weaker's hands slip.[11]

With the boys Joseph often played baseball and variations on quoits. He was known to create games with prizes, including booby prizes. On occasion, especially when he had beaten a challenger, he would say something like, "You must not mind this. When I am with the boys I make all the fun I can for them."[12]

So much for the athletic side.

Turn for a moment to his mind. It was a remarkable mind. Mother Smith records that he was "much less inclined to perusal of books than any of the rest of our children, but far more given to meditation and deep study."[13] Yet as he matured and as the weight of his calling came upon him he became an assiduous, hard-reading student, poring over the scriptures, even being appointed to go over them word by word, line by line, and make inspired changes. In addition to that he aspired to the ancient languages.[14] At Kirtland he set up a school in Hebrew with Joshua Seixas as the teacher. Six of the students had not even mastered English in its rudiments. The minutes say that the two outstanding students in that school were Joseph Smith and Orson Pratt, in that order.[15] The worst was Heber C. Kimball.[16]

Intellectual gifts fall into many categories. For convenience, let us consider four. First of all there is imagination, the ability to picture the concrete pictorially, vividly, in its possibilities and variations. This is the fund of creativity. Joseph Smith had a vivid ability to picture and, some would add, a dramatic propensity. He counseled that we should avoid, as he put it, "a fanciful and flowery and heated imagination."[17] He had the gift. But he did not abuse it.

Next is the ability to conceptualize; to understand principles, information, truth, and then (which isn't quite the same) to express them accurately, clearly, and, as need be, briefly. Joseph Smith, whatever his early tendencies and however he may or may not have shown up in school, had a brilliant conceptual ability both to see and to understand, to go to the heart of an issue and then to express it so that others would understand. Related to that is the admonition he wrote while he was for many months in isolation in Liberty. He wrote a letter, parts of which are in our Doctrine and Covenants (but part that is not included is equally profound).[18] He says: "The things of God are of deep import; and time, and experience, and careful and ponderous and solemn thoughts can only find them out. Thy mind, O man! if thou wilt lead a soul unto salvation, must stretch as high as the utmost heavens, and search into and contemplate the darkest abyss, and the broad expanse of eternity—thou must commune with God."[19]

That remarkable passage is in the context of his saying that often in our most important council meetings, classes, and gatherings we have been light-minded, "vain and trifling," and too often unconcentrated in our direction.[20]

Third is memory, the ability to retain what one learns and summon it at will for further use, implication, or application. Apparently Joseph had to learn by repetition, just as the rest of us do, for in 1823 Moroni came and repeated the same message four times, including quotations from scripture. Thus the Prophet heard them often enough and clearly enough to recognize differences from the King James version of the Bible.[21] Four times he had to hear the message. Many might suppose that one visit from such a heavenly visitor would be sufficient. On the contrary. Joseph listened. He remembered.[22]

We find evidence of his remarkable memory near the other end of his life, when he sat down with William Clayton and his brother Hyrum and dictated the revelation we now call section 132 of the Doctrine and Covenants. It is a long revelation—sixty-six verses, many of which are themselves long. Verse 19, for example, is over two hundred words. Some of the verses describe the conditions of the everlasting covenant in such terms as an attorney might use who had spent days thinking up every possible synonym, nuance, and contingency so that no loophole would remain. For example: "All covenants, contracts, bonds, obligations, oaths, vows, performances, connections, associations, or expectations, that are not made and entered into and . . . ." That's the subject of the sentence. Then there's the verb. Then a very long predicate.[23] To have written that after patient winnowing of the dictionary would be an achievement. Joseph Smith dictated it straight and, apparently, without a change. That is amazing enough. But then we learn from William Clayton that the Prophet declared that "he knew the revelation perfectly, and could rewrite it at any time if necessary."[24] Now, that is staggering! He had the essential core of that involved revelation so clearly in mind that he had full confidence he could restate it. He may have meant that he could dictate it in the exact words, and if this is so he was indeed gifted in that respect beyond normal mortal ability. But I think he meant only that the content was clear to him and it would not be lost if the written version were lost. That shows a remarkable memory.

Fourth is the ability to be simplicity-minded, and that's a gift. Not "simpleminded," but "simplicity-minded," having the ability to reduce elaborate ideas to a core center or essence. At the same time it is a gift to be able to see what other minds do not; to recognize implications, nuances, extensions of ideas that go beyond ordinary perception. Here again Joseph Smith was an original, for on the one hand in administrative and decision-making enterprises he went quickly to the heart of the matter with ingenuity and skill. But on the other hand, if required and asked to elaborate on a given doctrine or teaching he could do so and then would stretch the minds of all present.[25]

As to the overall quality of the written work of Joseph Smith, Arthur Henry King, a convert to the Church and a renowned English professor, has said that in his judgment the Prophet's account in Joseph Smith—History (see the Pearl of Great Price), which includes his account of the First Vision and the visits of Moroni, is among the sublime prose in world literature. The same scholar has also said that one may contrast that writing favorably with the more ornate but in many respects more shallow writing of

Oliver Cowdery, whose description of his feelings during the translation process and during John the Baptist's appearance is given at
the end of Joseph's account in the Pearl of Great Price. Compare
the two prose styles. In every way, Arthur Henry King observes,
Joseph Smith's is superior.[26]

We need not apologize at all for the language or structure or
form of the Book of Mormon. It is among the great books of the
world. It is to be placed side by side with those books which are
called canonical. There is a transparency, a brilliance, a white light
about its most spiritual elements that I do not find anywhere else.
It is a masterwork. Joseph Smith did not produce it and could not
have produced it.

For years it has been said that anybody who had lived in Western New York or anybody who would take the time could grind
out such "imitation scripture" himself. Hugh Nibley, becoming a
little impatient with that sort of nonsense, once had a class of Middle East students, all of them from the Palestine area or farther
East. At the opening of his class he said: "I am making a term
paper assignment. By the end of the semester I would like each of
you to write 522 pages having the following characteristics." And
then he outlined what the Book of Mormon has and is. So far he
has not received the assignment back. No man and no combination of men could have written that book except under divine inspiration.

I offer one other point, this from my own perspective. Take
section 93 of the Doctrine and Covenants—I leave out many other
sections of which the same could be said. In my considered judgment (and I have read a little in the philosophers of the world) this
section is superior in content to Plato's *Timaeus*. Plato may or may
not deserve the reputation of being the greatest philosopher of the
western world, which has been reiterated through many generations, but I say that Joseph Smith, as an instrument for receiving
and transmitting God's word, was more profound than Plato.[27] He
had the added advantage of the Holy Ghost.

Now let's turn to his temperament, to his emotional makeup,
to his dispositions. Early in his own account of his life he said he

had a "native cheery temperament."[28] Thank the Lord he did. It stood him in good stead. Many joined the Church, some from foreign lands and some from the United States, many out of New England with its conservative and sometimes rigid Puritanical traditions, others from movements such as the Quakers and the Baptists. They compared Joseph Smith with his brother Hyrum, and remarked that Hyrum seemed more in the image of what they thought a prophet should look like and behave like. He was, they meant to say, more sedate, sober, serious.[29] The Prophet, for all his sobriety under proper circumstance, was a hail-fellow-well-met, easily inclined to laughter, sociable, animated, the life of the party, and colorful in his use of language. That was disquieting enough for some that they left the Church. For instance, a family visited the Prophet when he was upstairs for a time translating—serious and tedious work. Then he came downstairs and began to roll on the floor and frolic with his little children. This family was indignant and left the Church.[30]

Not only did Joseph Smith have that temperament, but he found it difficult to abide opposite attitudes, especially when they arose from false traditions. On one occasion ministers came to him intent on tying him up in scriptural analysis, as they had bragged they would do. They kept trying to push him into a corner, but each time he not only had answers but also questions for them that they couldn't handle. Finally they became convinced it would be better if they left. As they went to the door, the Prophet preceded them. He went out, made a mark on the ground, and jumped. "Now gentlemen," he said, "you haven't bested me at the scriptures. See if you can best me at that." They went away much incensed.[31]

A man who had developed a certain falsetto came to Joseph. In our generation we are not familiar with this phenomenon, but in preaching without public address systems in those days some Methodists—for example, in the role of exhorter—would pitch their voices high and shout so loudly that it could be heard a mile away. Sometimes they prayed that way. One man with exactly that tone came and said, with a kind of supercilious reverence, "Is it possible that I now flash my optics upon a Prophet?" "Yes," the Prophet replied, "I don't know but you do; would not you like to wrestle with me?" The man was shocked.[32]

On one occasion a man of that same stripe, Joshua Holman, a former Methodist exhorter, was out with some other men cutting firewood for the Prophet when they were all invited to lunch at Joseph's home. When the Prophet called on Joshua to ask a blessing on the food, he set about a lengthy and loud prayer that incorporated inappropriate expressions. The Prophet did not interrupt him, but when the man was through he said simply, "Brother Joshua, don't let me ever hear you ask another such blessing." Then he explained the inconsistencies.[33]

"I do many things to break down superstition," he said.[34] At another time, he said, "Although I do wrong, I do not the wrongs that I am charged with doing."[35]

Joseph had a sense of humor. He sometimes joshed the brethren even in serious circumstances. An example is the time when a report spread that a man had sold his wife and the price was a bulleye watch. Riding his horse, Joseph Smith came across Daniel McArthur chopping wood. The Prophet greeted him, then said, "You are not the young man who sold his wife for a bull-eye watch the other day, are you?"[36]

On another occasion, with serious intent but humorous overtones, the Prophet dressed up in rough clothes, got on a horse and rode down to meet a group of converts who had just arrived from England. He stopped one of them who was heading for the town.

"Are you a Mormon?" the Prophet asked.

"Yes sir," said Edwin Rushton.

"What do you know about old Joe Smith?"

"I know that Joseph Smith is a prophet of God."

"I suppose you are looking for an old man with a long, gray beard. What would you think if I told you I was Joseph Smith?"

"If you are Joseph Smith, I know you are a prophet of God."

"I am Joseph Smith," the Prophet said, this time in gentle tones. "I came to meet those people, dressed as I am in rough clothes and speaking in this manner, to see if their faith is strong enough to stand the things they must meet. If not, they should turn back right now."[37]

It would seem that the Prophet spent half his time trying to convince the slow and sludgy people who had a little faith that God was indeed with him and with them;[38] and that he spent the other half alerting the Saints that a prophet is a prophet only when he is acting as such, which means when he is inspired of God.[39] The rest of the time he is a mere mortal—has opinions, makes mistakes, and in a general way of speaking has to put his pants on one leg at a time as every other man does. It was difficult to strike that balance. Some thought he was too human, some thought he was too prophetic. Both were wrong.

George A. Smith, a cousin of the Prophet Joseph Smith, was in girth, at least, a larger man. He weighed nearly three hundred pounds. One day they were discussing William W. Phelps as an editor. He had a gift as well as a curse for using language in an abrasive way, and in his editorials he managed to offend almost everyone. In his conversation with the Prophet, George A. Smith's evaluation was that Phelps had a certain literary zeal, and that as far as George A. was concerned he would be willing to pay Phelps for editing a paper so long as nobody else but George A. would be allowed to read it. At this, it is recorded, "Joseph laughed heartily —said I had the thing just right." And then he hugged him and said, "George A., I love you as I do my own life." George A. was moved almost to tears and said, "I hope, Brother Joseph, that my whole life and actions will ever prove my feelings, and the depth of my affection towards you."[40] On another occasion he gave George A. this bit of serious counsel: "Never be discouraged. If I were sunk in the lowest pit of Nova Scotia, with the Rocky Mountains piled on me, I would hang on, exercise faith, and keep up good courage, and I would come out on top."[41]

There is next the question whether in all of his attitudes the Prophet demonstrated appropriate humility and the very thing he taught in word, namely, compassion and forbearance and forgiveness. He is reported as saying that he had "a subtle devil to deal with, and could only curb him by being humble."[42] No braggadocio, no threats, no vainglorying. We do not have power over the adversary and his hosts except through the power of Christ, and we do not have such power save we are humble and receptive. What is humility? There are a thousand definitions, but it means at least acknowledging one's dependence on the Lord, acknowledging when and where one is not self-sufficient. Joseph, according to those who knew him best, was in that sense humble.

Here we are not talking about boldness—he had that; it is not the opposite of humility. We are not talking about willingness to endure in strength—he had that, and that too is not the opposite of humility. We are saying that Joseph did not manifest the debilitating pride that destroys humility. That is the witness left by several who knew him best.

Eliza R. Snow, who had heard of the Prophet and some very ugly things in that connection, happened to be at home one day when the Prophet called and visited with her family. "In the winter of 1830 and '31, Joseph Smith called at my father's," she wrote of this visit, "and as he sat warming himself, I scrutinized his face as closely as I could without attracting his attention, and decided that his was an honest face."[43] Later, after joining the Church, she was often in his home as a kind of babysitter and help for a time in Kirtland. She first admired him in his public ministry, saw him as a prophet, but not until she saw him in his own home, on his knees in prayer, and in his relationship with his children did her whole heart go out to him in admiration.[44] He was, she said, as humble as a little child.[45]

Was the Prophet an emotional man? In all the worthy senses of that word, the answer is yes. The tears sprang easily to his eyes, and this happened in varied situations. There is, for example, the occasion on which Parley P. Pratt returned to Nauvoo by boat, having been on a long mission, and the Prophet came down to greet him and just wept. When Parley could extricate himself he said, "Why Brother Joseph, if you feel so bad about our coming, I guess we will have to go back again."[46] He wept, too, at good-byes: the tears were flowing fast on the day he said good-bye to his family before he left for Richmond Jail. The Lord himself acknowledged this compassionate heart when he said in a revelation, speaking of Joseph, "His prayers I have heard. Yea, and his weeping for Zion I have seen, and I will cause that he shall mourn for her no longer."[47]

He characterized himself as "like a huge, rough stone rolling down from a high mountain; and the only polishing I get is when some corner gets rubbed off by coming in contact with something else."[48] He also called himself a "lone tree."[49] He had learned in Vermont that those maples that stood alone had to develop deep roots early; if they did not, the inevitable blast of winter storms would take them down. For all of his social sense, there were times when he felt deeply lonely. "O that I had the language of the arch-angel to express my feeling once to my friends," he said. "But I never expect to."[50]

"You don't know me," he said in the King Follett discourse. "You never knew my heart." And then this remarkable phrase, "I don't blame any one for not believing my history. If I had not ex-perienced what I have, I could not have believed it myself."[51]

In that loneliness, he had to keep to his own bosom (those were his words)[52] certain deep understandings the Lord had vouchsafed to him with the command that he not share them. "The reason," he once said, "we do not have the secrets of the Lord revealed unto us is because we do not keep them but reveal them . . . even to our enemies." Then he added, "I can keep a secret till Doomsday."[53] And so he did.

As an emotional and loving man, what kind of a home life did the Prophet have? Under the buffetings that relentlessly began with the Prophet's announcement of his first vision and continued until his death, it is miraculous that he had as much time at home as he did. He and Emma had nine children, of whom four died at birth and one at fourteen months. In the ache of her bosom at the loss of twins, Emma moved the Prophet to go and bring home twins, a boy and a girl, whose mother had died in that same week. Emma raised those children. The boy died at eleven months under the exposure he suffered the night the Prophet was mobbed in Hiram, Ohio—beaten, tarred and feathered, and left. The girl lived to maturity but never responded to the message of the gospel. Only in one instance did Emma bear a child in a home she could call her own, and that was David Hyrum, born after the Prophet's death.

And as for Emma in general, the certainty of the record is this simple: Joseph Smith loved her with his whole soul. And the corollary is, Emma loved him with her whole soul. She was "an elect lady."[54] She was not only a remarkable woman but, except for the difficulties that came with plural marriage, she was also a noble and glorious supporter of all the Prophet did, as Mother Smith indicated in her personal tribute.[55]

The Prophet's home life with Emma included prayers three times a day, morning, noon, and night.[56] It included her leading the family in singing. The "family" was always larger than Joseph's blood relatives—visitors from different places, immigrants needing temporary accommodation, and so on. Some came for a week or so, and some, like John Bernhisel, for three years. Being so commanded as "an elect lady," she compiled a hymnal, some of whose contents are still in our present hymnbook.

The Prophet Joseph helped Emma in taking care of the children and the domestic chores—building fires, carrying out ashes, bringing in wood and water, and so on. He was criticized more than once for that, some men thinking that was beneath his dignity. With kindly reproof the Prophet set them straight and counseled that they go and do likewise. The Prophet was neat, too. His axe was always carefully sharpened and properly placed after he had used it. His store of wood was always neatly stacked, his yard was well kept, until his death he was a farmer who earned much of what he was able to eat by plowing, planting, weeding, and harvesting.[57]

We have a glimpse of his sleeping ability from Lorin Farr, who observed that even in the Missouri persecution days, even under pressure—and of course he was then under the kind of pressure that leads to the worst fatigue—he could sit down at the base of a tree and almost instantly fall into slumber, but almost as instantly snap back to full and alert activity. That may have something to do with a clear conscience and the assurance that God is with you.[58]

He avoided, but could not wholly avoid, the tedious trivia of life. He did not like the clerical functions. He was less than enthusiastic about the commandment which came on the very day the

Church was organized that a record must be kept day by day and that in it all of the important events should be recorded.[59] But he complied. He had helpful scribes. He was patient with them, and they with him.

In a relaxed moment one day the Prophet turned to his secretary, Howard Coray, and said, "Brother Coray I wish you were a little larger. I would like to have some fun with you," meaning wrestling. Brother Coray said, "Perhaps you can as it is." The Prophet reached and grappled him and twisted him over—and broke his leg. All compassion, he carried him home, put him in bed, and splinted and bandaged his leg. Brother Coray later said, "Brother Joseph, when Jacob wrestled with the angel and was lamed by him, the angel blessed him. Now I think I am also entitled to a blessing." Joseph had his father give him the blessing, and his leg healed with remarkable speed.[60]

To Robert B. Thompson, his secretary, the Prophet said, "Robert, you have been so faithful and relentless in this work, you need to relax." He told him to go out and enjoy himself, to relax. But Thompson was a serious-minded man. He said, "I can't do it." Joseph responded, "You must do it, if you don't do it, you will die." One of the sorrows of Joseph's life was that Robert B. Thompson had a premature death, and he had to speak at the funeral.[61]

He learned to relax, and when chided for it he commented that if a man has a bow and keeps it constantly strung tight, it will soon lose its spring. The bow must be unstrung.[62] Somebody who saw him with his head down, pensive and deep in thought, said to him, "Brother Joseph, why don't you hold your head up and talk to us like a man?" The Prophet's response was, "Look at those heads of grain." The man looked out at the field of ripened wheat and saw that the heaviest sheaves, the ones full of grain, were bent down. The Prophet was implying that his mind was heavy laden.[63] But fortunately he could unleash.

Two other glimpses of his home life: When mistreated, he was inclined to "get even" by offering the hospitality of his home. That involved Emma and her talents in cooking. Often he invited people with little warning—"If ye will not embrace our religion, accept our hospitality."[64] There were times when the cupboard was bare. One day they had nothing to eat but a little corn meal. They made out of it a johnnycake, as it was called, and the Prophet offered the blessing as follows: "Lord, we thank thee for this johnnycake and ask thee to send us something better. Amen." Before the meal was over a knock came at the door, and there stood a man with a ham and some flour. The Prophet jumped to his feet and said to Emma, "I knew the Lord would answer my prayer."[65] He shared and shared until he was utterly impoverished.

Now a few comparisons: We have the testimony of Peter Burnett, one-time Governor of California, who had known Joseph Smith in the Missouri period, that he found him a man of great leadership gifts, a man who instinctively commanded admiration and respect.[66] Stephen A. Douglas whose title, "the Little Giant," was, one source claims, applied to him by Joseph Smith—the same Stephen A. Douglas who debated Lincoln and who aspired, as the Prophet predicted he would, to the Presidency of the United States—had many admiring things to say of Joseph during the Illinois period. He said he had independence of mind.[67]

Alexander Doniphan was the general who refused to shoot the brothers Smith in the Far West square as ordered, and who wrote to General Lucas, "I will hold you responsible before an earthly tribunal, so help me God."[68]

James W. Woods, the Prophet's last attorney, was with him on the morning of June 27, 1844. Never a Latter-day Saint, he observed that you could see the strength of Joseph Smith in his manner and dignity, but he added that you could see by his face alone that he was not a bad man.[69]

Daniel H. Wells, "Squire Wells," who heard Joseph speak twice in Nauvoo, was a kind of nineteenth century justice of the peace. He heard him speak on the principle that every son and daughter of Adam, sooner or later, whether in this life or the next, will hear the gospel of Jesus Christ in its purity and in its fullness and will have adequate option to choose it; and that those who accept it and live it, including the disembodied spirits who would have done so if they had had opportunity in mortality, will have the right and access to all the ordinances that are performed only in this life. How? By proxy. This man, trained in law and impressed by the justice of the Prophet's teachings, said, "I have known legal men all my life. Joseph Smith was the best lawyer that I have ever known in all my life."[70]

We have from Brigham Young a comment on Joseph's being different from Hyrum, and beyond the obvious comments is one to the effect that Joseph's ability, including his breadth of vision, was superior to Hyrum's.[71] An implication of this is that Joseph was more susceptible to the continuing impressions and revelations of God. That is, he did not become so rigidly bound to what had been given that he was unsusceptible to what yet had to be given. Yet that is a tendency. Claiming integrity, one can harden on past traditions and can thus become immune to living revelation. And the Prophet tended to judge men with that same openness: that is, not all cases are identical; each individual has his own special differences, and must be brought into harmony with the Lord in ways that recognize these differences. Again, this shows a mind that is not only open but also receptive; and not only receptive, but also obedient, even when the required response seemed to run counter to former assumptions and traditions.[72] This was an essential element for *the* revelator of our dispensation.

To summarize, in Joseph Smith we have a man who physically, intellectually, emotionally, and spiritually was a living human multitude. He was many men in one, as it were. Many of his gifts were balanced with others, and all in all he was a superb instrument with whom the Lord could and did work in the dispensation of the fulness of times.

# Joseph Smith and Spiritual Gifts

We have three classic scriptural statements about spiritual gifts: what they are, where they come from, and the spirit in which they are to be sought and manifested. Those three sources are Doctrine and Covenants section 46, Moroni chapter 10, which is also the last chapter in the Book of Mormon, and Paul's statement in 1 Corinthians 12. These three are interrelated and can be studied profitably by comparison.

If we go through the scriptures as history and make note of ways in which the Spirit of God has been manifested in the lives of individuals, we find at least thirty ways. In the account of these gifts in section 46 the Lord makes the statement, "to every man is given a gift," signifying, apparently, that each of us is entitled to at least one spiritual gift. The Prophet said elsewhere, "A man [he could equally as well have said "a woman"] who has none of the gifts has no faith; and he deceives himself, if he supposes he has."[1] Orson Pratt made the same comment in a different way. "No one," he said, "who has been born of the Spirit, and who remains sufficiently faithful, is left destitute of a spiritual gift."[2] One follows from the other. "No man can receive the Holy Ghost without receiving revelations," Joseph Smith explained. "The Holy Ghost is a revelator."[3]

Why spiritual gifts? The Lord says, "That ye may not be deceived seek ye earnestly the best gifts, always remembering for what they are given; for . . . they are given for the benefit of those who love me and keep all my commandments." And then a very happy phrase: "and him that seeketh so to do."⁴ So not only those who are fully living the commandments can hope for these gifts but also those who are trying, seeking. The warning is clear: "always remembering for what they are given."

Then comes the caution: Saints are to "ask and not for a sign that they may consume it upon their lusts."⁵

In the same revelation the Lord promises that "unto some" (the bishop, for example, and such others as are called to preside in the Church) "it may be given to have all those gifts."⁶ Elsewhere the Prophet said: "The gift of discerning spirits will be given to the Presiding Elder. Pray for him that he may have this gift."⁷ This is the precious, almost indispensable gift for any leader in the Church. But "unto some it may be given to have all those gifts [not just one, but all], that there may be a head."

With that as a premise, I have gone through the life of Joseph Smith and singled out instances in that life when these gifts were manifest. It is no surprise that he did, in fact, experience all the spiritual gifts.

With a desire to improve our awareness of spiritual possibilities and to increase our recognition of ways in which Joseph Smith was indeed a prophet of the Lord Jesus Christ, let us consider in serial fashion the more prominent though in some cases less well known experiences of the Prophet in this respect.

One of the first gifts Moroni mentions is that of "*exceedingly great faith.*" As section 46 puts it, "to some it is given by the Holy Ghost to know that Jesus Christ is the Son of God, and that he was crucified for the sins of the world."⁸ The Prophet Joseph Smith certainly had exceedingly great faith. We have the demonstration over and over of his coping with trials that sorely tested his endurance, his perseverance. We also have, at the outset of his ministry, his testimony of the effect the verse James 1:5 had on him. (One wonders whether James, when he wrote the verse way back in the first century, could have had any notion of the impact it would have.) The following two verses are similarly powerful: "But let him ask in faith, nothing wavering. For he that wavereth is like a wave of the sea driven with the wind and tossed. For let not that man think that he shall receive any thing of the Lord."[9] We are often willing to say what we would like to receive of the Lord, even what we would do *for* it, but we are not as eager to say what we will do *with* it once it is given. The Prophet proved himself willing on both counts.

In connection with that gift it is said, "To others it is given *to believe on their words*,"—"their" meaning those who have great faith—"that they also might have eternal life if they continue faithful."[10] Some people are gifted to know, and others are gifted to believe on what those people know. Or, to put it differently, some people have secondhand testimonies. My own conviction is that this is a preparatory gift. It is not sufficient unto itself. You cannot live and endure and overcome simply on the basis of believing the word of another. Sooner or later, and preferably sooner, you too will come to firsthand and direct knowledge for yourself.[11]

The Prophet did believe on the word of other trustworthy souls. He was sponsored and nourished and strengthened thereby. He pored over the records of the past until they became part of his nature. A study of his sermons, for example, on the question of how often he slipped almost inadvertently into the language of the New Testament, shows that a great deal of his thinking and feeling was conditioned in the phrases of Paul and also in the writings of John and other New Testament books.[12] The same would go for the Old Testament and such books as he himself became an instrument in translating. He trusted the revealed word and in that sense proved himself a believer second hand.

*The gift of prophecy.* This is the gift of anticipating future events. Elder John A. Widtsoe, after making a study of the Doctrine and Covenants, concluded that it contains nearly eleven hundred statements about the future.[13] If one extends beyond the Doctrine and Covenants to other scripture, to the personal promises the Prophet gave in blessings, to comments made in sermons, to his counsels in the midst of his own brethren and sometimes in private and sacred circumstances, and to predictions he wrote in letters, they would far exceed that eleven hundred.[14]

The Prophet said on one occasion that "the Lord once told me that if at any time I got into deep trouble and could see no way out of it, if I would prophesy in His name, he would fulfill my words."[15]

One can discern, therefore, times in his life when he almost despaired and when that state of mind was the symptom, or the background, of his uttering prophecy. In Kirtland, for example, in that period of mass apostasy when perhaps half of the Church members were falling away, including many of the Twelve, he rose in tears after prayer in a meeting one night and said, "I prophesy in the name of the Lord that those who have thought I was in transgression shall have a testimony this night that I am clear and stand approved before the Lord." Many in whom this prophecy was fulfilled bore their witness in later testimony meetings.[16]

Prophecy can be a burden as well as a blessing, for as a person commits himself in the spirit to a certain course of action or a certain counsel of the Lord, he is by that very process making himself responsible to do all within his power to bring it to pass. It was so in the case of Joseph Smith, as it was with Heber C. Kimball, who was perhaps the second most prophetic man in LDS history.[17] Often, even in trivial circumstances, Joseph slipped into a prophetic mode—as trivial, for example, as the question whether it was going to rain enough to wet people's shirt sleeves in the grove as they listened to a discourse, or whether they should break ranks while in a Nauvoo Legion parade and return to their homes.[18] He would sometimes say, "It will not rain," and he would sometimes say, "I prophesy that it will rain—you've only got a few minutes —go!"

To those who argued that there was no such thing as prophecy, ancient or modern, he would say (quoting John in Revelation 19:10): "The New Testament says that the testimony of Jesus is the spirit of prophecy. I am a servant of Jesus Christ. I have a testimony of Jesus. Therefore, I am a prophet."[19] Occasionally he tied his enemies into a logical paradox. He would say, "Have you discovered that there is no revelation? How?" They would say, "Does not the Bible end all revelation?" He would reply, "If so, there is a great defect in the book or it would have said so."[20] Pointing out that it takes revelation to know that there will be no more revelation, he once asked, "Have ye turned revelators? Then why deny revelation?"[21]

As a prophet he said things which to me are "keys that never rust." When he said, "I will give you a key that will never rust," he meant that what he would say would last in its power till the end of time. An example:

In the midst of the leadership struggle, the apostasy of a group in Nauvoo led by William Law and the claim of others to have special perogatives of leadership, he said, "I will give you a key that will never rust." This is a test. "If you will stay with the majority of the Twelve Apostles, and the records of the Church, you will never be led astray."[22] Not one offshoot group can pass that test. How many were on the stand, for example, at Nauvoo in August 1844, after the Prophet's death, when Sidney Rigdon wanted to be the guardian and, in effect, the leader of the Church? How many of the Twelve were on the stand when the decision was made to follow the Twelve? There were seven, a bare majority (John Taylor was recovering from his wounds, and four had not yet come back from missions to the East). Again and again, in Church history the Twelve in unity have made the revelatory decisions, under the prophet, which have been binding upon us all. And the records? Which records are most important? Likely, I suggest, the records of temple ordinances. We have them, we preserve them, and they are a mark of authentic transmission of divine authority and power to our day.

Joseph Smith made many prophetic statements that last to our day.[23] Some of them seemed preposterous at the time. Lillie Freeze recalls one such. "He said the time would come when none but the women of the Latter-day Saints would be willing to bear children."[24] In large measure this is already happening today—before our eyes. He said on another occasion that the Saints would be driven and would suffer, but they would go to the Rocky Mountains and there become a great and mighty people.[25] Other recollections of that prophecy do not say a great and "mighty" but a great and "wealthy" people who would be tried more with riches than they ever had been with poverty.[26] This too is happening before our eyes.

Joseph was prophetic in promises to individuals. "Your name," he said to Brigham Young, "shall be known for good and evil"— just as Moroni had said to Joseph himself.[27] And it is so. He said to Eliza R. Snow, "You will yet visit Jerusalem." She wrote it in her journal and forgot it. Forty years later it came to pass.[28] When death seemed near in the Carthage jail, Joseph uttered one of his last prophecies. To Dan Jones he said, "You will yet see Wales, and fulfill the mission appointed you before you die."[29] Dan Jones later helped convert over fifteen thousand people in Wales. "Have no fears, for you shall yet see Israel triumph and in peace," Joseph said to fifteen-year-old Johnny Smith, whose feet were bloody from drilling with the Nauvoo Legion.[30] He did.

There was a beautiful moment when Dimick Huntington in a shoe shop was working on the Prophet's boots. The Prophet recounted things Dimick had done for him, mostly physical and comforting things — rowing the boat across the Mississippi until his hands were blistered, carrying messages, and as the scriptures have it, "hewing wood and drawing water." The Prophet expressed gratitude and finally said to Dimick, "Ask of me what you will, and it shall be given you, even if it be to the half of my kingdom." Dimick did not want to impoverish the Prophet. He asked something else. "Joseph," he said with his whole soul, "Joseph, I desire that where you and your father's house are [meaning in eternity] there I and my father's house may be also." The Prophet put his head down for a moment as if in meditation, and then looked up. "Dimick, in the name of Jesus Christ, it shall be even as you ask."[31]

The father of Dimick was named William. One night the Prophet learned from Shadrack Roundy, who stood guard at his gate, that a mob was on the river. Shadrack Roundy's "rascal beater," which we would call a billy club, would not be enough against twenty men. The Prophet went down the street to William's house, woke him up, and said, "A mob is coming, counsel me." William said: "I know what to do. You climb in my bed. I'll go back and get in yours." That is what they did.

The mob came and dragged William out. Down by the river they discovered they had the wrong man. Their viciousness knew no bounds. In wrath, they "stripped him, roughed him up, tarred and feathered him, and herded him back into Nauvoo like a mad dog."[32] When he finally staggered into his own home the Prophet embraced him and said with all the power of his soul, "Brother William, in the name of the Lord I promise you will never taste of death." That prophecy was fulfilled.[33]

To be able so to prophesy in the name of Jehovah was both the blessing and the burden of Joseph Smith. "Brethren," he said— this is Wilford Woodruff's recollection—"I have been very much edified and instructed in your testimonies tonight, but I want to say to you before the Lord, that you know no more concerning the destinies of this church and kingdom than a babe upon its mother's lap. . . . This church will fill North and South America —it will fill the world."[34] Related to that, George A. Smith recalled hearing the Prophet once say "that we may build as many houses as we would, and we should never get one big enough to hold the Saints."[35]

*Discernment.* We have previously noted the Prophet's words: "The gift of discerning spirits will be given to the Presiding Elder. Pray for him that he may have this gift."[36] Discernment is the recognition of the spirit that actuates a person. "The way I know in whom to confide—God tells me in whom I may place confidence," the Prophet said.[37] Jesse N. Smith records, "I felt when in his presence that he could read me through and through."[38] Wilford Woodruff says that once he met him on the street. The Prophet took his hand, held him, and paused while he seemed to be searching the other man's soul. Then he said, "Brother Woodruff, I am glad to see you. I hardly know when I meet those who have been my brethren in the Lord, who of them are my friends. They have become so scarce."[39]

A man acting, as it were, as an undercover agent came to Nauvoo, tried to work his way into the good graces of the Prophet, then invited him out for a walk. On the crest of a hill the Prophet stopped, called him by name, and said, "You have a boat and men in readiness to kidnap me, but you will not make out to do it."[40] It was true. The man had planned to kidnap him, but instead he went away cursing. Joseph once wrote in a letter, "It is in vain to try to hide a bad spirit from the eyes of them who are spiritual, for it will show itself in speaking and in writing, as well as in all our other conduct. It is also needless to make great pretensions when the heart is not right: the Lord will expose it to the view of faithful Saints."[41]

Despite the presiding officer's discernment, Joseph Smith set up the law of witnesses, which requires that evidence and testimony must be used to prove a person's acts.[42] But the spiritual recognition that something is wrong or that something is right, he had. He once prayed to know whether a choir in Nauvoo was singing acceptable praises to God. The Lord made known to him that the director was immoral. Shortly the man resigned and left.[43] Joseph was discerning, although he trusted many beyond their trustworthiness—which perhaps was a function of what Brigham Young described as his "regarding everything according to the circumstances of the case and every person according to the intrinsic worth."[44] Brigham himself once said, in the spirit of the Prophet: "If you have the spirit of God you can discern right from wrong. When a man is not right, even though his language is as smooth as oil, there will be many queries about him, he will not edify the body of the Saints." And Brigham added, "I give this to you as a key."[45] Yes, Joseph discerned.

*Dreams.* Some dreams result from pressure, from diet, from anxiety. Some psychological research indicates that we all need to dream, that our mental health depends upon it. But there are also dreams sent of the Lord. It is one of the spiritual gifts. Being warned in a dream, Joseph fled with Mary and Jesus into Egypt. The wife of Pilate had a dream that gave her much anxiety. She pleaded with her husband not to condemn Jesus.

Joseph Smith had prophetic dreams, as he once indicated to Levi Hancock. Levi started on a mission, was out one night, had a terrible night of nightmares, and returned in fear. "Don't let that trouble you," said the Prophet. "I have had dreams as bad as you ever had. You do as I now tell you to and you will come out all right." Levi recalled that Joseph then "gave [him] to understand how the Comforter would comfort the mind of man when asleep."[46]

Then there was the dream—the ugly, ominous dream—at Nauvoo. He dreamed of William and Wilson Law. They had cast him into a pit, a pit higher than his head, so that there was no way for him to climb or spring out of it. Shortly both of them were attacked by serpents and were dying. They cried out for his help. All he could say was, "I would help you if I could, but you have made it impossible for me to help."⁴⁷ This dream was all too authentic. William and Wilson Law were leading spirits in the *Nauvoo Expositor* and in the meetings of conspiracy that culminated in the Prophet's death.⁴⁸

*Visions.* There are visions in open daylight, waking visions, as we say; and visions that occur in the night. Did Joseph have visions? "It is more than my meat and my drink," he once said, "to know how I shall make the Saints of God to comprehend the visions that roll like an overflowing surge, before my mind."⁴⁹ Frustrated at times in his effort to teach, though there is abundant testimony of his effectiveness, he sometimes felt, as he said to John Taylor, as if he were "shut up in a nutshell."⁵⁰ Whenever he countered the traditions that people had accumulated, some would "fly to pieces like glass."⁵¹

He said in frustration, talking about the Saints: "There has been a great difficulty in getting anything into the heads of this generation. It has been like splitting hemlock knots with a corn-dodger for a wedge and a pumpkin for a beetle."⁵²

Now, that's nineteenth century! Hemlock knots are tough. If you had a wedge made of cornmeal like a pancake, and if you tried to drive it in with a pumpkin, you know how well you might do at splitting hemlock knots. That's how effective he felt his teaching sometimes was. And yet the Lord did reveal and unfold line by line the whole plan. "I have the whole plan of the kingdom before me," he said, "and no other person has."⁵³ Everyone else had parts, fragments, pieces. But over the training period the Lord gave Joseph Smith, he received it all.

Some of his visions were panoramic. He said of Doctrine and Covenants section 76 on the three degrees of glory, "I could explain a hundred fold more than I ever have of the glories of the kingdoms manifested to me in the vision, were I permitted, and were the people prepared to receive them."⁵⁴ A hundred times more than the present length would be more than the full length of the Doctrine and Covenants.

More knowledge stored itself in his mind, I believe, than in any intellect since the time of the New Testament. And yet he said, "I am not learned, but I have as good feelings as any man."⁵⁵

Learned he was not in the standard bookish and university sense. But taught by the greatest teachers in the universe he was. It will not do if one is speaking of him in his maturity to say that Joseph was "an ignorant farm boy." He had by that time become a very informed, enlightened, and divinely taught man. "The best way to obtain truth and wisdom," he said, "is not to ask it from books, but to go to God in prayer, and obtain divine teaching."[56] He also said that "an open vision will manifest that which is more important."[57] But in another connection he said that the Lord "always holds himself responsible to give a revelation or interpretation of the meaning thereof."[58]

As for the principles he had that placed him in communion with ancient worthies, John Taylor said he was as familiar with the ancient prophets and apostles and patriarchs, including those of the Book of Mormon, as we are with one another. Examples: He said one day of his brother Alvin, "He was a very handsome man, surpassed by none but Adam and Seth."[59] In the spirit of instruction in Nauvoo, Joseph described Paul: "About five foot high; very dark hair; dark complexion; dark skin; large Roman nose; sharp face; small black eyes, penetrating as eternity; round shoulders; a whining voice, except when elevated and then it almost resembles the roaring of a lion."[60] How did he know that? I've known a few scholars who claim to be the world's leading experts on Paul. One man, I suspect, knows more than they. That is Paul. Apparently he is one who taught Joseph Smith.

Doctrine and Covenants 128 tells of some of the ancient worthies who manifested themselves to the Prophet Joseph, declaring their keys and glories and dispensations and making possible the welding of authorities in this dispensation.[61] He knew Peter, he knew James, he knew John. He knew Adam and Eve. He knew Abraham. He knew Enoch. He knew the Twelve who were on the American continent. "He seemed to be as familiar with these people as we are with one another," said John Taylor.[62] He had visions of the past as well as of the future. As a seer, he knew things about the past that are not part of our own scripture, but which he spoke of in discourse.

This indeed was a visionary man in the best and highest sense.

*Tongues.* Did the Prophet Joseph Smith ever speak in tongues? He did. Brigham Young met him for the first time in Kirtland. They had a meeting. Brigham was called upon to pray, and in the course of this prayer spoke in an unknown tongue. When he and the others rose from their knees and were seated, the Prophet addressed them: "Brethren, this tongue that we have heard is the gift of God, for He has made it known unto me, and I shall never oppose anything that comes from Him. I feel the spirit that Brother Brigham has manifested in this gift of tongues, and I wish to speak myself in the tongue that it will please the Lord to give me." After then speaking for a time in that tongue, Joseph declared: "Brethren, this is the language of our father Adam while he dwelt in Eden; and the time will again come, that when the Lord brings again Zion, the Zion of Enoch, this people will then all speak the language which I have just spoken."[63]

As for interpreting tongues, on an occasion when the Prophet was subpoenaed and was leaving to attend the trial, he was met at the door by a sister named Sarah who spoke to him. The Prophet listened intently. When she was through, he said, "You need not fear for me, as Sister Cleveland says I shall have my trial and be acquitted."[64] She had spoken in tongues and prophesied. He was tried, and he was acquitted. It is recorded by John Nicholson that the Prophet once gave a blessing to Orson Pratt in the course of which he spoke in an unknown tongue, naming several worlds which he, as a servant of the most High, should visit in order to minister to their inhabitants.[65] One of the cries of this generation is the need for a religion for the Space Age, a religion that isn't earthbound but that takes account of the vast universe we now know about. Through the Prophet Joseph Smith was revealed a religion for the Space Age, for the cosmos, for the whole universe. That brought division and opposition into his life.

*To heal, and to be healed.* These are separate gifts. The Prophet was called upon, over and over, to administer—sometimes with oil, sometimes not—to those who were sick, both in his own family and beyond it. On the occasion now known in LDS annals as "the day of God's power" (July 22, 1839), he himself arose from a sick bed of cholera and went across the river to Montrose, Iowa.[66]

Dozens were instantaneously healed that day. His journal says only, "Many of the sick were this day raised up by the power of God."[67] He does not add, "and I was the major instrument." We learn from others' journals that he led that procession of faith.[68]

He counseled his brethren in this matter. He pleaded with them, according to Parley P. Pratt, to "cease to minister the forms without the power."[69] How one does that without having mighty faith, I do not know.

There were times when he had to give repeat blessings. Jedediah M. Grant had dyspepsia, perhaps what we would now call a stomach ulcer. He would feel better for a time when the Prophet administered to him, and then the pressures would arise, things would eat on him, and he would be back in the same condition. The Prophet one day said, "Brother Grant, if I could always be with you, I could cure you."[70] This is testimony of the serenity of soul of the Prophet, and of the faith of Jedediah. Joseph's personal presence might have overcome this uneasiness of stomach.

Was the Prophet himself faithful sufficiently that he was ever healed? Yes—repeatedly. He once was poisoned and then vomited so violently that his jaw was thrown out of joint. He was immediately administered to and healed.[71] In another experience, this time with his brother Hyrum, at the end of the Zion's Camp march, he prophesied that because the Camp was not repentant and not living as a modern Camp of Israel should, some of them would die. One account says, "like sheep with rot"—a terrifying statement.[72] Thirteen died. In spite of his prophecy, Joseph yearned to heal them. He and Hyrum tried, but they had no sooner laid their hands on the sufferers than they themselves were smitten with cholera. They felt its ravages, fell down prostrate together, and prayed for deliverance. Even at that moment, Mother Smith was praying for them.[73] In prayer they asked for a testimony that the Lord would relieve them and that healing would come. Within minutes they arose free of the disease which, in other cases, was fatal.

*To have knowledge and to teach it, to have wisdom and to teach it.*[74] I believe this involves four spiritual gifts. It is possible for a person to know much, and yet be ineffective in teaching. What is the distinction between knowledge and wisdom? I know of no final scriptural definition. But, clearly, just to have extensive knowledge —as the Prophet once said, "being puffed up with correct (though useless) knowledge"—is no great blessing.[75] It is about as vain as pride in other areas. But wisdom is something else. Wisdom is the insight that comes out of genuine, firsthand experience.

Some write that Joseph Smith seemed to possess, as Edward Stevenson put it, "an infinity of knowledge."[76] Wilford Woodruff wrote that Joseph Smith was "like a bed of gold concealed from human view," and that, as with Enoch's, only God could comprehend his soul.[77] Jedediah M. Grant said that "Joseph could take the wisest Elder that ever travelled and preached, and, as it were, circumscribe his very thoughts,"[78] and others said that he would teach and testify with such power that no other man in the kingdom could match him. All that gives us indication of his wide knowledge.

A promise was given him in 1833 that he would have "power to be mighty in testimony."[79] This promise was brilliantly fulfilled. Loren Farr said to his grandson, "Oh, my son, I have sorrow that you will never hear the Gospel of Jesus Christ taught in power."[80] He meant that Joseph Smith was dead and gone, and that though there were giants in the kingdom, none of them could command the power of heaven as he had, standing between heaven and earth in witness, and in testimony.

Yes, he had knowledge. And he taught.

He was not a natural orator. Others of the brethren were more eloquent in the flowery sense; Sidney Rigdon certainly was, Parley P. Pratt was. Others were more orderly and systematic; Orson Pratt was. Others were more practical in their counsel; Brigham Young was. But it is a testimony to the Prophet's greatness that all of these, each superior in one way or another, yet sustained him as the greatest prophet of all time, apart from Jesus Christ himself.[81]

A final word on his wisdom. "I made this my rule: When God commands, do it."[82] That took him all the way to Carthage—and to the glories of the eternities beyond.

*To recognize the diversities of operations and the differences of administration.* It is possible that the term "diversities of operations" refers to the recognition of the movements, the trends, the activities, the ongoing processes of history, recognition as to which are centered in the light, in the influence of the living God, and which are simply of man, and which, if any, are from the lower regions. "Lying spirits are going forth in the earth," the Prophet said. "There will be great manifestations of spirits, both false and true."[83] The adversary always sets up his kingdom in opposition to the kingdom of God.[84] The multiplicity of variegated religions in our generation is, indeed, a sign of the times.

Joseph Smith felt and taught, and it is the testimony of this Church, that as Latter-day Saints we must recognize that the Lord's Spirit has worked upon all generations and all cultures. This is confirmed by the First Presidency statement of February 15, 1978, wherein they mention some of the great religious leaders, such as Mohammed and Confucius, as well as ancient philosophers. These, they say, received a portion of God's light.[85] While often condemned for being "exclusive," Latter-day Saints belong to the one Church that has the capacity to retain its roots and still relate to, and eventually embrace, all mankind, sifting through the error and offering the truth in its place.

The Prophet Joseph had that kind of expansive soul. "We should gather up all the good and true principles in the world," he said, "and treasure them up, or we shall not come out true 'Mormons.' "[86]

*To have communion with the heavens, to see both angels and spirits.* Section 107 of the Doctrine and Covenants says that the Melchizedek Priesthood, in holding the keys of the spiritual blessings of the Church, is to have the privilege of holding communion with the general assembly and church of the Firstborn.[87] Who are they? Apparently they are the most righteous, who have filled their missions on earth and are now serving worthily in the spirit world or have inherited celestial glory. Did Joseph have communion with them while he was on earth? Yes. The only other man in LDS history who enjoyed a comparable richness of communion was Wilford Woodruff, who seemed to have had that gift from birth, and who seemed to live as if with one foot in the spirit world and one foot in this one. Only Wilford Woodruff could say to a brother as he went down the street in Salt Lake City, "Brother John, it's good to see you," and then could add as an afterthought, "You know, I don't think I've seen your father since he died."[88]

Finally, though there are other gifts, I mention the working of miracles. Someone asked the Prophet once, "What was the first miracle Jesus performed?" He answered, "He made this world, and what followed we are not told."[89] *Miracle* is the term we use for the operation of divine power beyond our understanding. It is not a violation of law. Every miracle that Christ performed, including the creation of the earth, was executed in harmony with eternal principles. We will one day know that whatever we call miraculous was, in fact lawful.

Joseph was promised that upon him would be laid much power.[90] When someone who had known him was asked to name the greatest miracle she had seen in the first generation of the Church, she replied that it was Joseph Smith.[91] The Prophet was a God-made man. It will never do to say, as critics are beginning to say, "This man was a genius." So saying, they wish to reduce a most remarkable movement to its leader, its founder, and, as they believe, its origin. True, he was a genius, he was a brilliant man. It takes a brilliant man even to comprehend, let alone to write, as he comprehended and wrote, the glorious insights that came to him, even granting that they came from the Lord. He was a man of superb intelligence.

Nevertheless, that does not explain Mormonism. What explains Mormonism is that Joseph Smith at his greatest, as a prophet, was not merely Joseph Smith. He was a prophet, made so by the power of God. He was a modern miracle.

# Joseph Smith and Trials

Early in this dispensation, a revelation was given in which the Prophet was addressed as follows: "Be patient in afflictions for thou shalt have many; but endure them, for lo, I am with thee, even unto the end of thy days."[1]

Near the end of his life, the Prophet wrote: "Deep water is what I am wont to swim in. It all has become a second nature to me."[2] In the same epistle, he said, "The envy and wrath of man have been my common lot all the days of my life." But, he added, "I feel, like Paul, to glory in tribulation; . . . for behold, and lo, I shall triumph over all my enemies, for the Lord God hath spoken it."[3]

On his deathbed in Nauvoo in 1840, Father Smith said to his wife, Lucy, "You are the mother of as great a family as ever lived upon the earth." On that same occasion, Father Smith gave a blessing to each of his assembled children, blessings that not only prophesied but also reflected the monumental struggle that the Prophet and those around him had had and yet would have to endure.[4] In a revelation given in 1829, the year before the Church was organized, Joseph had been admonished, "Repent and . . . be firm in keeping the commandments . . . and if you do this, behold I grant unto you eternal life, even if you should be slain."[5] One month later both Joseph and Oliver were addressed with this counsel: "And even if they do unto you even as they have done unto me, blessed are ye, for ye shall dwell with me in glory."[6] Speaking of enduring persecution in a Christlike way[7] rather than of merely surviving our trials (which most of us manage to do), the Prophet said: "Those who cannot endure persecution, and stand in the day of affliction, cannot stand in the day when the Son of God shall burst the veil, and appear in all the glory of His Father, with all the holy angels."[8] This is an interesting test each of us might apply to himself.

"Many of the elders of this Church will yet be martyred," Joseph said on one occasion,[9] and one wonders whether the long shadow of his own martyrdom was in his mind at that time. Persecutors did do unto him and his brothers as they had done unto the Lord. They fought, they vilified, they attacked. They perceived him as a threat to them, and they did all within their power to stop him. Someone has suggested that the worst difficulties that came to the early Church arose from its clash with other organized religions. That, I think, is a half-truth. The Church did suffer immensely from what could be called "officialdom" in the religious world, and it suffered more in political and social areas. By all odds, the opposition that was the most difficult and painful and hurtful to the Church was that which arose from apostates.[10]

The ancient ministry of Christ faced betrayal from within, and it was so also in the early days of this modern dispensation. A revealing conversation once occurred between Joseph Smith and a brother named Isaac Behunnin. He had seen men involved in the quorums and in the high spiritual experiences of the kingdom who had subsequently become disaffected, and it was a mystery to him why they had then devoted their zeal and energy to attacking the Church. He said to the Prophet: "If I should leave this Church I would not do as those men have done. I would go to some remote place where Mormonism had never been heard of, settle down, and no one would ever learn that I knew anything about it." The Prophet immediately responded: "Brother Behunnin, you don't know what you would do. No doubt these men once thought as you do. Before you joined this Church you stood on neutral ground. When the gospel was preached, good and evil were set before you. You could choose either or neither. There were two opposite masters inviting you to serve them. When you joined this Church you enlisted to serve God. When you did that you left the neutral ground, and you never can get back on to it. Should you forsake the Master you enlisted to serve it will be by the instigation of the evil one, and you will follow his dictation and be his servant." Happily, Brother Behunnin was faithful to his death.[11]

What Joseph said there became a genuine description of case after case. To name a few: William McClellin, John C. Bennett, William Law, and to some degree Thomas B. Marsh. Up until the Nauvoo era every one of the Prophet's own counselors, with the sole exception of his brother Hyrum, either betrayed him, went astray, faltered, or failed in some way. Some, glorious to report, found their way back. Orson Hyde, not a member of the First Presidency but one of the Twelve, under oath endorsed terrible things said against the Church and the Prophet, of which he later repented.

But many remained bitter in their opposition to the end. "If it were not for a Brutus," Joseph said in 1844, "I might live as long as Caesar would have lived."[12] There was more than one! So, much enmity came from within and Joseph struggled as the revelation warned him he would: "If thou art in perils among false brethren. . . ."[13] That is only the beginning.

Think for a moment of Joseph's physical setbacks. In chapter two we noted his leg operation early in life. He had a slight limp ever after and could not be enlisted in the state militia in Missouri because of that injury.[14] On that awful night, at the Johnson home in Hiram, Ohio, when he was dragged out and his body was bent and twisted by strong men, they left him with back sprains from which he never recovered. That night they tried to poison him with aquafortis (nitric acid) and as he clenched his teeth to prevent the vial from going in his mouth, one of his teeth was broken.[15] It was never properly cared for, and there was a slight lisp in his speech after that.[16] On one occasion he was beaten with guns in a wagon until he had an eighteen-inch-circumference bruise on each

side.[17] More than once he faced the diseases of the time but over-
came them, and he was even smitten with cholera at the end of the
Zion's Camp march.

In all of this Joseph struggled both to endure and to overcome.
That is the tension we all face. What must we simply go through,
and what, through our faith and worthiness, can we overcome? He
was never completely free of physical strains and, again, never
really free of the pressures of the Presidency. He was indeed in deep
water.

Throughout life, in his own family some deep cuts and wounds
came to him. For example, several of his children died at birth or
soon after. He speculated—he did not say it was a doctrine of the
Church—that perhaps some of the choice children born into this
world and then taken so quickly were "too pure, too lovely" to live
on this wicked earth, so the Lord took them.[18] On the other hand,
he once observed that he did not like to see a child die in infancy,
because it had not yet, as he put it, "filled the measure of its creation and gained the victory over death.[19] Apparently the Prophet
did not tell all he knew about this subject, but it may well be that
the plan makes provision for such children to obtain the requisite
mortal experience later (in post-millennial circumstances?) and
make the necessary choices that lead to exaltation.[20]

A woman recorded years later that, at the Prohet's request,
her mother "lent" one of the family's twin little girls to him and
Emma to assuage their loneliness at the loss of their own children.
Joseph called her "my little Mary." In the morning he would come
just after breakfast, pick up the child, take her home to Emma for
most of the day, then bring her back in the evening. When he was
late in returning the child one day the mother went to the Prophet's home and found him dandling her on his knee and singing to
her, as she had been fretful. The next morning she handed him
Sarah, the other baby. Strangers could not distinguish one from
the other, but Joseph did. He took a step or two, stopped, turned
back, and said, "Oh no, this is not my little Mary." She gave him
Mary instead, and he smilingly carried her away.[21]

Many have observed that Joseph's love for children was remarkable, that he seemed to find deep happiness playing with a

child on his knee, or helping one across a muddy field, or picking flowers to give to children, or wiping away their tears.[22] I believe that the response of those children, and we have record of many, to him is one of the lasting witnesses of the nobility of his soul. Children are not easily deceived. Many have described how they felt in his presence. How he loved little children!

In Nauvoo, preaching was almost always done out of doors because there was no adequate inside accommodation. (The temple was unfinished.) There was sometimes the problem of order and decorum. Often people stood to listen, sometimes on the benches of their wagons drawn up near the speaker. Occasionally the younger people would move out behind the dais or to the side, which was a distraction. Those charged with the responsibility for order, the ushers and others, could be very severe to those young people. The Prophet chided those who went too far. "Let the boys alone," he would say, "they will hear something that they will never forget."[23] "May God bless you, my little man," he said to ten-year-old Amasa Potter as he took the boy by the hand. "You have a great work to perform in the earth, and when you are in trouble think upon me and you will be delivered."[24]

Another of the Prophet's trials in the home related to the burdens imposed on their marriage by his persecutors, burdens that Emma too had to carry. Often they would think they had a moment of peace, and then there would come the rude shock at the door: another lawman, another lawlessman, another subpoena, another cry, another warning.[25] At one point two little girls were charged with keeping their eyes open for anyone who came within a block of the house. They would rush to the house and say, "Someone suspicious-looking is coming." Sometimes the Prophet would leave, and sometimes he would hide, and sometimes the person would turn out to be a friend who looked disreputable, such as bearded, long-haired Porter Rockwell. Joseph would scoop up the children and run out and say, "Now, now, he's not all that bad, is he?"[26]

Then there were the endless legal entanglements. Brigham Young said that Joseph had forty-six lawsuits.[27] The standard LDS statement is that he was acquitted from all these. It is true in most cases that he was, but in some he was convicted. There was a charge, for example, in the state of New York that he was guilty of casting out an evil spirit. The trial was held and he was found guilty. The judge then observed that there was, to his knowledge, no ordinance against that, and he would have to be set free![28]

Often the basis of the complaints charged against Joseph, especially in the early days, was about the same as the ancient Christians faced, as recorded in the book of Acts: "You have set the neighborhood in an uproar."[29] So he had. But how could he help it? Light always stirs up darkness. That is an eternal law. Some dark souls were stirred up to murder, to the assassinations at the Carthage Jail. Only then was Joseph free from his enemies and their lawsuits.

It seems to me symbolic that Willard Richards, speaking to calm the Saints after the word was out that Joseph and Hyrum had fallen, said, in effect, Do not make any rash moves, do not seek vengeance, leave all of this to the law, and *when* that fails, leave it to God. Notice, not "*if* that fails" but, "*when* that fails, leave it to God."[30] It failed. A trial was held of five men charged with involvement in what Dallin H. Oaks and Marvin S. Hill call the Carthage Conspiracy, but they were all acquitted.[31] None of those involved at Carthage was ever brought to earthly justice. So be it. Eternal justice will take care of it.

Of the Prophet's many trials, surely one of the most severe was the five months' imprisonment—four of them in the infamous Liberty Jail. There is something ironic in that name. Part of the reason why he was there was Sidney Rigdon's "Salt Sermon," which had been delivered in June 1838, in which the speaker had used as his text Matthew 5:13. He applied it to the prominent dissidents in the Church—they were like the salt that has "lost his savour," and were henceforth "good for nothing, but to be cast out and to be trodden under foot of men."[32] On Independence Day, July 4, he gave an even stronger speech that defied enemies of the Church, whether individuals or mobs, and vowed the Saints would retaliate against any further oppression. Contention escalated, mob violence spread, a militia besieged the Saints' city of Far West, and Joseph and other leaders were taken prisoner.

During those cold winter months in Liberty Jail—December through March—Joseph did not have a blanket. He wrote to Emma and pleaded for one. She had to reply that in his absence William McLellin, formerly one of the original Twelve Apostles and now a vicious antagonist, had stolen all the blankets from his house.[33] Several times the jailers administered poison to the prisoners, and as a mean joke, on one occasion they tried to feed them with human flesh.[34] There were no sanitary facilities except the slop bucket, and there was very little light.

Joseph was not alone; his brother Hyrum and four other brethren were with him. In some respects that was an added affliction, as he saw their sufferings too. The reports piled up of cruelties inflicted on the Saints—the whippings, the beatings, the rapes, the plundering of homes and farms, and finally the enforced exodus to Illinois in dead of winter, leaving bloody marks in their footprints on the snow. These weighed heavily on the souls and the hearts of these men in prison for conscience' sake.[35]

Joseph's personal trials were one thing; those of the Saints he loved were another. He prayed for an answer from the Lord to the two questions: "How long, O Lord, wilt thou witness these things and not avenge us?" And the other question, "Why?" Why must the Saints suffer so?[36]

To the first the Lord answered that in due time "a generation of vipers" would receive their due.[37] But to the second there was no full answer, except the answer that Job received, and the admonition to trust: "The Son of Man hath descended below them all. Art thou greater than he?"[38]

The full explanation of trials is never that we have sinned. The full explanation is that we are sometimes called on to go through affliction. The Missouri Saints had not fully lived up to their covenants, and the Lord made that known to Joseph. Part of their difficulties, therefore, was deserved.[39] But that will not take care of that great sum of man's inhumanity to man that remained. What happened at Haun's Mill, for example, was undeserved.[40]

Joseph had to learn forbearance, had to learn forgiveness. He also had to learn vigilance. He would say, in effect, "If ever I am in such a situation, I will help you. I will not say I can do nothing for you. I *can* do something for you and I will."⁴¹ That's an echo and a reversal of President Martin Van Buren's response to him in Washington. But he prophesied also at times that there would be repentance and that some who had most hated us would become our most beloved. And so it was.

Patience he had to learn. Pain he had to endure.

We can talk, then, of the spiritual burdens he bore: how he was called over and over again to impose sacrifices on himself and on others when he would rather have not. Here is an example. Place: Kirtland. Commandment: Build a temple. The question: How? Stands here Brigham, stands here Joseph. How will we build a temple? They review the names of every Latter-day Saint they can think of who has ability in construction, and there isn't anyone who can do it. Then Joseph Young says: "Well, I know a man up in Canada; he's excellent in construction work. His name is Artemus Millett; but of course he's not a member of the Church."

At that point Joseph turns to Brigham: "Brother Brigham, I give you a mission. You are to go to Canada. You are to convert Artemus Millett. You are to bring him back to Kirtland with his family and tell him to bring at least a thousand dollars in cash." It is a testament of the mettle of Brigham that he said, "All right, Brother Joseph, I'll go." Go he did. He did convert Artemus Millett and his family. They did come to Kirtland with the thousand dollars.⁴² Brother Millett oversaw the construction of that temple and later the Manti Temple. That is one of the up-against-the-wall impossibilities—perhaps hundreds of them in the Prophet's life—that both wrenched his soul and stretched it.

Even when he saw, secondhand and at a distance, what the Saints had to bear, he broke into tears and privately went into prayer. In such a case, at the Nickerson home in Toronto he became aware of a young girl named Lydia Bailey. By the tender age of eighteen, she had had one husband and two children. Her husband had abandoned her and both children had died. Why? Joseph went to the Lord. Then he met with Lydia. An outpouring of the Spirit ensued, and Joseph made promises to her that out of her affliction there would come into her life such strength as she could not now comprehend. "The Lord, your Savior, loves you, and will overrule all your past sorrows and afflictions for good unto you." She had a role to play in the redemption of her family that she could not fully understand. The promises came to fulfillment.[43]

How he suffered in the witness of how his family suffered! "My father," cried out his six-year-old son, "My father, why can't you stay with us? What are the men going to do with you?" And then the boy was thrust from him by the sword.[44] The Prophet cried unto the Lord, "Bless my family."

The one journal we have that he wrote in his own handwriting over a daily period of time was on a missionary trip north into Canada. It reflects two preoccupations. Over and over the journal turns into a prayer: "Oh, God, establish thy word among this people." And the other: "Lord, bless my family."[45]

Calm times were rare, but we find in the records here and there a day of family peace, especially at Christmas. On Christmas Day 1835: "Enjoyed myself at home with my family, all day, it being Christmas, the only time I have had this privilege so satisfactorily for a long period." The Prophet recorded the following for Christmas morning 1843: "This morning, about one o'clock, I was aroused by an English sister, Lettice Rushton, widow of Richard Rushton, Senior (who, ten years ago, lost her sight), accompanied by three of her sons, with their wives, and her two daughters, with their husbands, and several of her neighbors, singing, 'Mortals, awake! with angels join,' &c., which caused a thrill of pleasure to run through my soul. All of my family and boarders arose to hear the serenade, and I felt to thank my Heavenly Father for their visit, and blessed them in the name of the Lord. They also visited my brother Hyrum, who was awakened from his sleep. He arose and went out of doors. He shook hands with and blessed each one of them in the name of the Lord, and said that he thought at first that a cohort of angels had come to visit him, it was such heavenly music to him."[46]

Joseph was stretched to do things that he was not by his own reckoning fully equipped to do in the temporal sense. One promise says, "In temporal labors thou shalt not have strength, for this is not thy calling."[47] Yet he was required to introduce advanced ideals—not just dreams, but actual structures: in economics, the law of consecration; in politics, the Council of Fifty; in social thought, plans for communities, and for their very city design with the temple at the center—thus he was, among other things, a city planner. Educationally, he established the School of the Prophets and the University of Nauvoo, and the school instructions that are outlined in sections 88 and 109 of the Doctrine and Covenants involve processes for the expansion of the knowledge and skill and power of his faithful band. How could a man be stretched to that?

It is one thing to be spiritual adviser and to bring forth inspiration. But it is quite another thing to take a melting-pot group of converts from all over the world and introduce instantly plans for their temporal welfare—and he always taught that you could not totally separate the temporal and the spiritual. To do that he had help. The Lord raised up men all around him. He needed all that and more. "The burdens which roll upon me," he said once, "are very great."[48]

In the community setting he referred to "the contraction of feeling." (He thought this was one of the absolute marks that apostasy had occurred.) "It is one evidence that men are unacquainted with the principle of godliness, to behold the contraction of feeling and lack of charity."[49]

He talked to the Relief Society, the faithful women to whom he paid high tribute. "As you increase in innocence and virtue, as you increase in goodness, let your hearts expand, let them be enlarged towards others; you must be long-suffering, and bear with the faults and errors of mankind. How precious are the souls of men! The female part of the community are apt to be contracted in their views. You must not be contracted, but you must be liberal in your feelings."[50] And he warned them against gossip, warned them against the unruly tongue. He said, "God does not look on sin with allowance, but when men have sinned, there must be allowance made for them. . . . The nearer we get to our heavenly Father, the more are we disposed to look with compassion on perishing souls; we feel that we want to take them upon our shoulders, and cast their sins behind our backs."[51]

Many came to him bearing burdens of sin and pleaded for him to intervene for them, to help them. There were also those who came and pleaded for other kinds of help. It was as if he could not avoid being servant of all. How would it be, for example, to be sound asleep, the doorbell rings, and there stand before you two black women. They have travelled over eight hundred miles, mainly across the countryside, not daring to use the highways lest they be apprehended. They have escaped from some who have threatened their lives. They are both converts to the Church.[52] What can they do? Where can they go? Joseph calls Emma down. "Emma, here is a girl that has no home. Haven't you a home for her?" "Why, yes, if she wants one." Jane, one of the two, stayed with them for the rest of the Prophet's life. She records what it was like to be involved in the prayers of that family, and that she was treated not as a slave and not as a servant but as one of the family.[53]

The Prophet's role as a judge and as mayor of Nauvoo and the head of the Nauvoo Legion required him to discipline the legionnaires and render judgment as the mayor. Anthony, a black, had been selling liquor in violation of the law—to make it worse, on the Sabbath. He pleaded that he needed money urgently to buy the freedom of his child held as a slave in a southern state. Said Joseph: "I am sorry, Anthony, but the law must be observed, and we will have to impose a fine." The next day Joseph gave him a fine horse to purchase the freedom of the child.[54]

The pressure of love, of caring about the Saints and wanting them to receive and follow the will of the Lord, was another major part of Joseph's load. Sometimes—even as early as the mid-1830s— he would have welcomed deliverance into the next world, leaving the kingdom in the hands of others. "Oh! I am so tired," he told his friend Benjamin Johnson, "so tired that I often feel to long for my day of rest. . . . Bennie, if I were on the other side of the veil I could do many times more for my friends than I can do while I am with them here." Yet there was an ambivalence. "If it were not for the love of you, my brethren and sisters, death would be sweet to me as honey."[55] Before leaving on the Zion's Camp march, he charged Brigham Young, "If I fall in battle in Missouri I want you to bring my bones back [to Kirtland] and deposit them in that sepulchre—I command you to do it in the name of the Lord."[56] In 1835 he said, "I supposed I had established this church on a permanent foundation when I went to Missouri, and indeed I did so, for if I had been taken away, it would have been enough, but I yet live, and therefore God requires more at my hands."[57]

Many threats on the Prophet's life were empty; some were not; to all he exhibited a fearlessness that may have been related to his readiness to shed the burdens of mortality. Someone asked him, "How do you dare think you are safe in the midst of your enemies?" Once he answered, "Because the children are praying for me."[58] During two weeks in hiding with the Prophet, tramping through the woods, William Taylor, age nineteen, asked, "Don't you get frightened when all those hounding wolves are after you?" Joseph answered: "No, I am not afraid; the Lord said he would protect me, and I have full confidence in His word."[59]

It was at the home of his wife's nephew Lorenzo Wasson that he was accosted by Sheriff Reynolds of Missouri and Constable Wilson of Carthage, Illinois. Without legal process they pointed their pistols at his chest and threatened to shoot him if he stirred. Joseph, baring his breast, said "I am not afraid to die. Shoot away. I have endured so much oppression, I am weary of life; and kill me, if you please. I am a strong man, however, and with my own natural weapons could soon level both of you."[60] Confidence? Beyond the ordinary.

In Far West, Missouri, the mob lined up about 3500 men, preparing to attack and destroy every Mormon there. There were between two and three hundred, including two or three Jack-Mormons (in those days that term meant a Mormon sympathizer). Aware of those three, a man came with a flag of truce and said, "We're going to wipe you out, but we understand that a few of you aren't Mormon: they can come with us." Those non-Mormons decided they would stay. Then said the Prophet to the man with the white flag, "Go back and tell your general to withdraw his troops or I will send them to hell."[61] John Taylor, who was present that day, said years later, "I thought that was a pretty bold stand to take."[62] That may be the understatement of the nineteenth century. The man went back with his flag, and the militia withdrew.

That same courage, faith, and endurance as was exhibited in the open land around Far West was shown in cramped and confined conditions in Nauvoo. Edward Hunter, who became a Presiding Bishop, records that he and the Prophet would hide in the little attic in his house, which still stands in Nauvoo. I say "little" because they couldn't even stand up there. They went up through a trapdoor, but by then they were over the rafters and under the roof, so they had to double down and sit. They were often many hours in that exact setting. There the Prophet wrote section 128 of the Doctrine and Covenants, a rhapsody—in an attic. In that same attic he said to Edward Hunter one day, "I know your genealogy, you are akin to me, and I know what brought you into the Church; it was to do good to your fellow men, and you can do much good."[63]

The sheer separation from his loved ones; the inability to speak, which he met by writing; the cooped-up feeling which because of his spontaneity and makeup he despised—all those things compounded to make life difficult. And yet he could write inspired, rejoicing literature. "Brethren, shall we not go on in so great a cause? Go forward not backward. Courage, brethren; and on, on to the victory."[64] He was not discouraged.

When he asked for peace of soul in moments of great anguish, like us he did not always receive the Lord's full explanation.[65] The demand that the Lord explain to us in detail why it is necessary for this or that—that demand takes us a step beyond genuine faith. If we are close enough to the Lord and if we have the assurance that we are filling our missions as appointed, it should not come as any great shock or surprise that we sometimes walk in affliction. That is the program. In a measure that is what we came to face and to endure in righteousness.

So Joseph was simply given assurance, the whisper of peace, the "Be still, Joseph, and know that I am God."[66] Or again, the serenity that does not assure you anything by way of, Where am I? or, Where am I going? but only, "You're on track, murmur not—all will work out in the end."

The Prophet had to endure and not know why or when. Along the way he had premonitions. "May I borrow that book?" he asked at the home of Edward L. Stevenson, in Pontiac, Michigan, in the early 1830s. The book was titled *Foxe's Book of Martyrs*.

When he returned it to Mother Stevenson in Missouri, he said, "I have prayed about those old martyrs." These were men and women who had literally given their blood and their lives for the testimony of Jesus. They were people of various faiths and backgrounds, but allegiance to their conviction meant death, usually in horrible forms. When he returned the book, he said: "I have, by the aid of the Urim and Thummim [perhaps the seer stone], seen those martyrs. They were honest, devoted followers of Christ, according to the light they possessed, and they will be saved."[67] Why would he have been preoccupied with that? Perhaps he anticipated that he would be numbered among them.

Again and again he had promises that his life would be prolonged to fill a certain mission. "Thy days are known," he was told in Liberty Jail, "and thy years shall not be numbered less."[68] What is that? A statement of fatalism? No, for we have contemporaries' recollections as to his statements on this: from Lyman Wight, that "he would not live to see forty years," and from at least two sources that speak of about five years—one of them giving the conditional "if I listen to the voice of the Spirit."[69] The revelation "Thy days are known . . ." was given in late March 1839. He was shot in Carthage on June 27, 1844, five years and three months after that.

During the last few months of his life, Joseph seems to have had a sense of urgency which in our day would be called a sense of living on borrowed time. In that period he laid upon the Twelve the burdens he had carried for so long, and he rejoiced at the relief it gave him. "Now the responsibility rests on you," he told them. "It mattereth not what becomes of me."[70] He did not fear death, he anticipated it, but he often said that he wanted to give his life in a way that would matter.[71] On a Sunday, a beautiful day, Benjamin Johnson records, they were sitting in the dining room and in came two of his children "as just from their mother, all so nice, bright and sweet." Joseph said, "Benjamin, look at these children. How could I help loving their mother; if necessary, I would go to hell for such a woman."[72] There is the truth about the legend that has grown up. Joseph Smith, so far as the evidence leads, never said (a) "Emma is going to hell," or (b) "I'm going to go to dig her out." He said, "I would go to hell for such a woman," meaning, "I feel strongly and deeply toward my wife." The distinction is clear.

Then he said to Benjamin something about other children. They had had a joint experience wherein he had blessed twenty-six in a row and had sensed what they would face in the trials of life and had concentrated his faith to seal upon them a blessing. In consequence he was weary when he had finished, and Jedediah M. Grant noted that he turned pale.[73] The Prophet had another anxiety, one that involved his beloved family. Of his four living children, the oldest was but thirteen, the oldest boy eleven, and another child was on the way. The record is clear that he was profoundly concerned about his family. He embodied the Abrahamic desire for children, honorable, loyal, faithful children, and certainly he would be leaving his own children in tender years and in critical circumstances. There is some evidence that the Prophet had a premonition of his eldest son's leading away a portion of the Latter-day Saints and thus creating a division in the family as well as in the kingdom he was living and dying to establish.[74] That must have pierced the Prophet deeply. He might well have chosen to live on for the sake of his family. That choice was denied him.

"Emma," he said on that last morning, according to one account, "can you train my sons to walk in their father's footsteps?" She replied, "Oh, Joseph, you are coming back." She couldn't believe he was not: he always had before. "Emma" — he repeated the same question. "Joseph, you are coming back." And the third time.[75] He left with such reticence that reportedly he went all the way back a third time to say good-bye to his children.

Yes, the Prophet Joseph Smith was a superb example of enduring and overcoming trials.

# Joseph Smith and the Kirtland Temple

How early in the Prophet's consciousness did the idea germinate that God would require the building and dedicating of temples and would reveal his ordinances to be performed in them? One way of reading our history is that the first and last revelations in the Doctrine and Covenants that Joseph received concerned the temple, though at first he may not have fully understood this. When the promise about priesthood which is part of section 2 of the Doctrine and Covenants[1] began to be fulfilled through John the Baptist's conferral of priesthood authority, Joseph Smith and Oliver Cowdery were told, "and this shall never be taken again from the earth until the sons of Levi do offer again an offering unto the Lord in righteousness."[2] Oliver Cowdery's wording of that statement is "that the Sons of Levi may yet offer an offering unto the Lord in righteousness."[3] The Prophet later came to understand that this offering relates to the temple.[4]

Elijah is a character whose life and promises apparently were reviewed when Moroni taught the Prophet over successive years. The passages about Elijah in the book of Malachi were quoted to the Prophet at least four times in two successive days in 1823. Somehow the hearts of the fathers would turn to the children and the hearts of the children to the fathers. And this was a key or power which Elijah would reconfer.

Kirtland became the preparatory location for the full restoration of those keys and ordinances. It was a revelatory moment when the Prophet was told that a house must be built, the exact dimensions were spelled out,[5] and he was told that it must be built by the sacrifice of the people—meaning, among other things, that it would not be easy—and that great blessings depended upon the completion of that work. The Church at the time was feeble, struggling, impoverished.

Since the Prophet and the other New York Saints had come to Kirtland, divisions and misunderstandings had developed. A meeting he attended was influenced by the "peepings and mutterings," as it were, of false spirits. Philo Dibble recalled that Joseph said, "God has sent me here, and the devil must leave here, or I will."[6] After counsel and ministration, there came a reunion of faith and understanding, and the Saints were given a revelation on how to discern the Spirit of the Lord and other spirits.

The core questions the Prophet asked then and later are still applicable today. "Is there any intelligence communicated?" Just babbling or speaking in an unknown tongue is not a communication of truth. Only when it is interpreted by a proper spirit is it so. So, "Is there any intelligence communicated?"[7] The other question: Is there anything indecorous in the experience? The bouncing, the violent movements, the hysteria that sometimes attended what people thought were "religious experiences" were condemned by the Prophet as not of God. God's Spirit is a refining and glorifying spirit, not a demeaning one.[8]

The Prophet had begun to establish the orders and patterns of Church organization, as he had been taught them, when the commandment came to build a temple. Financially the people were in severe straits. Sickness was not uncommon. Just to obtain the basic means of survival was difficult for most of the Saints. Nevertheless, soon "great preparations were making to commence a house of the Lord."[9] But in early June 1833 another revelation came in which the Saints were told, "Ye have sinned against me a very grievous sin, in that ye have not considered the great commandment in all things, that I have given unto you concerning the building of mine house."[10]

What was the "very grievous sin"? Apparently it consisted in not considering in all its aspects the commandment to build a temple, a failure to keep the commandments that were designed to prepare the Saints for a great spiritual endowment. What would solve this problem and bring about the endowment "with power from on high"? "It is my will," said the Lord, "that you should build a house. If you keep my commandments you shall have power to build it."[11] Less than two months later, on July 23, 1833, the cornerstones of the Kirtland Temple were laid.

It is instructive to observe here the Lord's warning as to the results of *not* keeping his commandments, words we may take as of general application. "If you keep not my commandments, the love of the Father shall not continue with you, therefore you shall walk in darkness."[12] Note that in this passage *love* is made a synonym for *light*, and darkness follows the absence of love. It seems to me that the scriptures show such a close kinship if not identity between light and love in the divine equation that it is impossible to have the one without the other.[13]

Of the building of the Kirtland Temple, Elder Boyd K. Packer has written: "The temple committee and others were soon busily occupied in obtaining stone, brick, lumber and other materials; funds were solicited; labor was donated for the construction; and the sisters provided food and clothes for the workers. The cost of the temple is estimated at $200,000, a very large sum in those days."[14] Several of our historians, Wilford Woodruff included, felt that though the Nauvoo Temple cost much more, it did not require the same level of sacrificial effort. The Kirtland Temple was an unprecedented sacrifice, and it was met with an unprecedented divine outpouring.

The Saints already had many active enemies in the Kirtland area, and when they learned of the intent to build a temple they vowed that it would never be finished—they would see to that! Hence, as the work progressed, enemies made attempts to prevent it. George A. Smith records that for every one man working, the brethren sometimes had three men guarding, some of them armed with pistols.[15] Nevertheless, the work went forward. The Prophet himself, not a skilled workman, could contribute at least his energy and muscle. Wearing his old smock he went into the stone quarry and with his bare hands helped to quarry the stone. By careful organization it was arranged that each seventh day, in this case every Saturday, every wagon the Saints had in the Kirtland area was summoned to haul stone to the temple site. Artemus Millett, a convert from Canada, supervised the construction. Truman O. Angell was the brilliant and inspired architect.[16] He planned and organized every element of the building.

As to the preparatory events, just to lay the cornerstones under crisis conditions was a major problem. Twenty-four Melchizedek Priesthood holders were required for the purpose, and at the time there apparently were not that many in the Kirtland area. Accordingly a few young men of fifteen and sixteen had their ordinations to the higher priesthood hastened, as they were made elders specifically for the purpose. A few older men, somewhat infirm, served as officers in the ceremonies.[17]

The Lord's house is a house of order, and the Prophet Joseph Smith had received a revelation as to the order even of laying cornerstones. Years later, at the laying of the cornerstones of the Manti Temple, Brigham Young arranged (and he said this was according to instruction) that the first stone be laid at the southeast corner, the point of greatest light, and at high noon, the time of the greatest sunlight.[18] All that is to remind us, we would assume, that the temple is indeed a house of light where the heavenly and the earthly combine.[19]

Several people who lived in Kirtland during the temple-building period have left us their accounts. One was Mary Elizabeth Rollins Lightner, then a young convert. She and her mother were living in Kirtland, and when she discovered the whereabouts of one of the rare copies of the Book of Mormon in that city, she went to the owner's home and asked to borrow it. He agreed, and she read it so avidly that he let her retain it for that purpose. About the time she finished reading it, the Prophet visited her home and, seeing the book on the shelf, recognized it as the one he had given to the present owner, Brother Morley. He was most impressed by young Mary, gave her a blessing, and told her to keep the book—he would give Brother Morley another copy.[20]

Mary and her mother went a few evenings later to the Smith home, where others were already assembled. Soon Joseph came in and they held a meeting, the people mostly sitting on boards put across chairs. The Prophet began addressing the group, but after a while he stopped speaking and remained silent. His countenance changed, and he became so white that he seemed transparent. He stood looking intently over the congregation. Finally he spoke. "Do you know who has been in your midst tonight?" Someone said, "An angel of the Lord." And Martin Harris said, "I know, it was our Lord and Savior, Jesus Christ." The Prophet put his hand on his head and said, "Martin, God revealed that to you. Brothers and Sisters, the Savior has been in your midst tonight. I want you all to remember it. There is a veil over your eyes, for you could not endure to look upon Him."

Then they knelt in prayer, which he led. His prayer was so long, Mary records, that several of the people rose and rested and then knelt back down to endure to the end. "Such a prayer," she said, "I have never heard before or since. I felt he was talking to the Lord, and the power rested upon us all."[21]

Later the Prophet gave a blessing to this dear sister. She became one of the faithful who in her ninety-plus years of life endured incredible trials for the faith.[22]

I recount the above story about one of many prayer meetings —John Murdock records several, Eliza R. Snow still others[23]—to show that the outpouring of the Spirit which sometimes attended the Prophet's words was but a foretaste of what was to come through the sacrificial building of the temple.

We have also the testimony of Zera Pulsipher, who was a convert to the Church at this time. He said that when old Father Smith came into the temple (presumably this would have been after its completion, but perhaps it also was before) he looked just like an angel.[24] We have spoken often of the Prophet's likenesses, but the venerable, aged father of the Prophet, seasoned and mellowed through much affliction, was a man who commanded the respect of the Saints. The Prophet often put him in charge of fast meetings, and in those days they held them quite often on Thursdays, people putting away their implements, leaving their work where it was and gathering in the spirit of fasting for testimony meetings. In such meetings prayers were often offered, both in private and in public, for the completion of the temple. And one of Father Smith's frequent petitions was that it would be fulfilled upon that temple as on the Day of Pentecost; that is, that the Spirit of God would descend upon it as a rushing, mighty wind, accompanied by tongues of fire. In due time that prayer was answered.[25]

Another witness to this period was a man named Daniel Tyler. He understood from the earliest Kirtland days that the priesthood which was bestowed in order to give ordinances the efficacy of authority had several branches and ramifications; that the patriarchal priesthood ultimately was the most inclusive and important priesthood, which could only be conferred in a sacred place; that exaltation, as it became clarified in subsequent revelations—which priesthood holders and their wives could only receive together—was in effect the extending, magnifying, and intensifying of the patriarchal priesthood throughout the expanding of eternal lives; and that God himself is the sovereign patriarch.[26]

Hints of that understanding came at Kirtland, but not until Nauvoo did the full scope of the patriarchal priesthood, the temple, and temple marriage become common knowledge to the Saints.[27]

We turn to a brief outline of the actual dedicatory services. Naturally, everyone who had done anything to help with the temple would want to be there at the dedication; and many others who might have been slow or critical or distant would still, out of curiosity, want to be present. The actual capacity of the room is variously estimated. One count of those who came that morning is that there were over 930.[28]

The Prophet had said that if children who would be orderly and were willing to sit on their parents' laps wanted to come, they could come. That suggestion caught on. It is reported that in the opening session there were two persons in each seat.[29]

The Prophet had held meetings to prepare the Saints, and especially the priesthood brethren, for what was to come. He told them that they must come in purity, come having studied and pondered prayerfully the revelations given on the subject.[30] In section 88 of the Doctrine and Covenants the Lord said the temple was to be a house of glory, a house of order, a house of prayer, a house of fasting, a house of God. Some specific commandments accompany those general ones.[31]

First, those coming into the temple were to be solemn, they were to cast away all light-mindedness. Light-mindedness, in the dictionary sense, is a lack of seriousness, and in the present context can include such attitudes as lack of interest in, making light of, betrayal of, flippant or frivolous approach to, even a ridiculing of, sacred things. Nowhere in the scriptures is lightheartedness condemned, nor again does scripture anywhere forbid a genuine, gentle humor that shows an appreciation for the foibles of ourselves and others. But light-mindedness clearly is inappropriate for Latter-day Saints, especially in the temple setting. In spite of the admonition, however, some found themselves upset, not thinking, for example, that it could be appropriate that men should wash one another's feet in the name of the Lord. They thought "some mischief was going on."[32] The Saints had been warned: be solemn, avoid light-mindedness.

Second, a series of commandments in section 88 warned the Saints to come as far as possible purified, to sanctify their hearts and hands, to cleanse their lives, to be clean in preparation for bearing the vessels of the Lord.[33]

Third came an admonition to study, in effect to read the revelations and to ponder and pray over them. On one occasion, as the climactic promise, the Prophet said to the brethren, "Brethren, all who are prepared, and are sufficiently pure to abide the presence of the Savior, will see Him in the solemn assembly."[34] What a promise!

So between nine hundred and a thousand people assembled early in the morning of March 27, 1836,[35] the Prophet and other authorities of the Church on the stand, and the dedication services began. The Saints had begun gathering at about 7:00 a.m. Joseph the Prophet presided, and Sidney Rigdon conducted. President Rigdon first read two of the Psalms—the ninety-sixth and the twenty-fourth. Then the choir sang a hymn, written by Parley P.

Pratt, called "E'er Long the Veil Will Rend in Twain." President Rigdon offered an opening prayer. The congregation then sang a William W. Phelps hymn called "O Happy Souls Who Pray."

President Rigdon then gave a sermon, based on Matthew 8:20, where the Master says: "The foxes have holes, and the birds of the air have nests; but the Son of man hath not where to lay his head." He expanded on that theme and gave it a modern interpretation: Anciently the house of the Lord in Jerusalem had been left desolate, the priesthood had become apostate, and Jesus himself had had to drive out of the temple the money changers, abusers, and blasphemers, saying: "It is written, My house shall be called the house of prayer; but ye have made it a den of thieves." But now, following the dedication, the Kirtland Temple would be the house of the Lord.[36] The address was appropriate and memorable, and President Rigdon spoke at length. There followed the sustaining of Joseph Smith as Prophet and Seer, and then the hymn, "Now Let Us Rejoice." That ended the morning service.[37]

A brief intermission followed, twenty minutes, long enough for a few of the sisters to take care of their children. But hardly anyone left. The proceedings then resumed with a hymn, a short talk by the Prophet, and the sustaining of Church leaders in more detailed fashion than is normally employed today. When another hymn had been sung, the moment arrived for which the congregation had waited.

The Prophet arose and gave the dedicatory prayer, a prayer which has been the pattern for all subsequent dedicatory prayers for temples down to the present. That prayer, which now constitutes section 109 of the Doctrine and Covenants, was given the Prophet by direct revelation. That was a puzzlement to some of the Saints. Strange that God, to whom we pray, should give a revelation telling the Prophet what to pray! But so crucial was that prayer, and so important, that it was given word for word through revelation. And it is magnificent! Students of Hebrew who know little of Latter-day Saints and less of temples comment that this prayer seems to partake of the Hebraic dualism, the balancing of phraseology and the insights of ancient Israel, that it has echoes and kinship with the prayer fragments we have in the Old Testament relating to the temple of Solomon. And so it does. That is to be accounted for on the ground that the ultimate source of temple worship is not man but God.

"O hear, O hear, O hear us, O Lord," the prayer finished, "that we may mingle our voices with those bright, shining seraphs around thy throne."[38]

With the prayer completed, the choir sang that magnificent hymn by William W. Phelps, "The Spirit of God." The dedicatory prayer was accepted by vote, and the sacrament was administered. Then came testimonies from the Prophet, Don Carlos Smith, Oliver Cowdery, Frederick G. Williams, David Whitmer, and Hyrum Smith.

Finally came the thrice-repeated Hosanna Shout—the first time, so far as I know, that it was used in this dispensation. The Prophet taught them how to do it, and they did it, "sealing it each time with amen, amen, and amen."[39] A shout! Does God want us to shout?

The hymn, written with the light of understanding, says, "We'll sing and we'll shout with the armies of heaven, Hosanna, hosanna to God and the Lamb." Meaning what? Anciently, crying "Hosanna!" with palm branches raised up was, in effect, a two-way reaching. On the one hand it was a plea: "O, save us"—a plea for redemption. On the other hand—as it was in the hearts of those who welcomed Jesus triumphantly into Jerusalem—it was a plea that he enter, that he come; it was an invitation that Christ accept and visit this holy house.[40] To put it in still another way, out of their depths the congregation expressed their need for Christ, and from the same depths they prayed for him to come. That was done in a shout with the raising of their arms in prayer.

Eliza R. Snow records this remarkable detail. One mother had been turned away at the door because her child was so small, only six weeks old. No one felt that he could endure through the entire day. But Father Smith welcomed the woman and said, "You come, and I promise you all will be well." Psychologists today tell us that children have two instinctive fears (all others they learn): one, the fear of loud noises; the other, the fear of falling. But when this mother rose to join in the Hosanna Shout, the six-week-old child pushed back his coverlet and joined in the shout.[41]

Immediately after the hosannas the Spirit of the Lord descended upon Brigham Young and he spoke in tongues, while another Apostle, David W. Patten, arose and gave the interpretation, then himself gave a short exhortation in tongues. Although there exists hardly a note about the content, these messages were, in essence, words of admonition and of divine approval. The Prophet then arose and left his personal blessing on the congregation, and the service ended at just a little past 4:00 p.m.[42]

What occurred in Kirtland following the dedication was something like a jubilee. The fact that every Saint who could had participated in the dedication either in person or in secondhand awareness drew the Church together into oneness. So intense was that feeling for some days and even weeks that many present thought the Millennium had come, that all tribulation and temptation was past. Such peace was in their hearts that they had no will to do evil. None of the standard battlements were in their lives. The Prophet had to warn them more than once that all they were experiencing was of God but that, soon enough, opposite experiences would come—the struggles with the adversary and with darkness would be renewed—and that they would know again all the trials that are at the core of saintliness. This was difficult for them to believe.[43] They went from house to house, for example, men, women, children, and would meet together, almost as we do on a beautiful Christmas morning, and would share their impressions, their experiences, each one having his own to report. And often the visitors would say, "I have a blessing for you, Brother," and would bless the other. And the person receiving would say, "I now have a blessing for you," and he would bless the visitor.[44]

Outside the temple, there were both Church members and nonmembers who sensed that something sacred was happening. Even little children. For example, Prescindia Huntington recalled: "On one occasion I saw angels clothed in white walking upon the temple. It was during one of our monthly fast meetings, when the saints were in the temple worshipping. A little girl came to my door and in wonder called me out, exclaiming, 'The meeting is on the top of the meeting house!' I went to the door, and there I saw on the temple angels clothed in white covering the roof from end to end. They seemed to be walking to and fro; they appeared and disappeared. The third time they appeared and disappeared before I realized that they were not mortal men. Each time in a moment they vanished, and their reappearance was the same. This was in broad daylight, in the afternoon. A number of the children in Kirtland saw the same." When her fellow Saints returned from the temple that evening and reported that during the meeting someone had said that "the angels were resting down upon the house," Prescindia understood.[45]

Some said there was a light—some used the word *fire*—that emanated from that building, and that at night it still seemed to be illumined. Others, even nonmembers, feeling this outpouring, this Pentecost, were caught up in the waves of love and light.[46] It seemed almost bitter contrast that Joseph should have to say to the Twelve in one of their meetings: "God will feel after you, and He will take hold of you and wrench your very heart strings, and if you cannot stand it you will not be fit for an inheritance in the Celestial Kingdom of God."[47]

How prophetic! Nine of the original Twelve became embittered in varying degrees by that wrenching that eventually came. But in the meantime, and before that darkness, there was more light.

The journals of many who were living in Kirtland at the time describe their activities in this period. They record things like this: that a time or two the Prophet would ask them to come, after fasting, and meet late in the day in the temple, and then would say, "We're going to be here in worship all night." He would instruct them as to the proper order for the meeting, and appropriate prayers would be offered. And then he would tell them to pray silently and then rise and speak as they were impressed by the Spirit.[48] Some spoke prophetically and in tongues, some rose to say they had heard heavenly music, and others rose and said, "I, too, heard it." These were celestial choirs, literally.[49] And there was the remarkable meeting in which a man and a woman arose spontaneously on the impression of the Spirit, sang in beautiful harmony in language they did not understand to a "song of Zion," beginning and ending each verse together, and then sat down.[50]

We would do well to ponder the harmony of soul that is presupposed in such an experience. Perhaps that is one way in which the promise of the Lord could be fulfilled that we shall one day "see as we are seen and know as we are known."[51]

Records of that day speak of remaining in meeting through the night, no one tiring, no one falling asleep, feasting on what the Prophet called the fat things of the Spirit. The effect produced by these was, in many of the Saints, overwhelmingly faith-promoting. But there were some who, instead of being lifted and inspired, felt that somehow this kind of thing was not what was to be expected — as if they had expected either more or less than this.[52] Shortly after these developments, some left the Church.

During the dedication service angels were seen. Elder Heber C. Kimball testified that "an angel appeared and sat near . . . Joseph Smith, Sen., and Frederick G. Williams, so that they had a fair view of his person." In the evening meeting that day, "the beloved disciple John was seen in our midst by the Prophet Joseph, Oliver Cowdery, and others."[53] The Apostle Peter also was named.[54] Eliza R. Snow, herself something of a master of language, wrote: "No mortal language can describe the heavenly manifestations of that memorable day. Angels appeared to some, while a sense of divine presence was realized by all present, and each heart was filled with joy inexpressible and full of glory."[55]

In fulfillment of a promise by Joseph Smith, George A. Smith arose in the evening meeting and began to prophesy. "A noise was heard like the sound of a rushing, mighty wind, which filled the Temple, and all the congregation simultaneously arose, being moved upon by an invisible power; many began to speak in tongues and prophesy; others saw glorious visions." Joseph recorded: "I beheld the Temple was filled with angels."[56]

Oliver B. Huntington later recalled: "Father Smith started up and spoke aloud, 'What's that — is the house on fire?' Some one answered by asking, 'Did not you pray, Father Smith, that the Spirit of God might fill the house as on the day of Pentecost?' "[57]

Now a word about the aftermath. Among the programs established in the midst of the Saints was what was known as the Kirtland Safety Society—which, ironically, turned out to be unsafe. Thwarted by an unexpected refusal of a state charter, its leaders reorganized the society as a joint stock company that would issue notes. Like many other banks of the time, it probably had inadequate reserves in specie (most of its assets being in land holdings), so that when redemption of its notes was sought in increasing quantities it was obliged to shut off payments in coin. Meantime a spirit of speculation developed and spread rapidly across the nation, and in the financial crisis that ensued when the bubble burst, hundreds of banks were closed.

It has been said that no part of man's anatomy is more sensitive than his pocketbook. The speculative spirit had become rampant among the Kirtland Saints, and many of them saw this time as their opportunity—perhaps even their blessing—to become wealthy. They took risks, they made foolish decisions. Holding notes from the Kirtland bank, some were bereft of all their meager savings when it failed. Many were terribly bitter as a result. Wrongly, they placed the blame upon the head of Joseph Smith. They failed to separate his roles as a man and as a prophet and to realize that from the start there had been no prophetic promise of success, much less a guarantee. Seeing its downward course, the Prophet had withdrawn from its leadership early in the summer of 1837. Actually the bank's failure brought him greater economic loss than anyone else. Not only had he bought more shares than any other investor except one but also, apparently in an effort to prevent the bank from failing, he sold property in Kirtland and also obtained three loans.[58]

The trial that came, as had been prophesied, had its effect in purging. It purged the Church of some who had been fair-weather members, and it purged many of the faithful of their more greedy and selfish impulses.

For many years, scholars critical of the Mormon historical past assumed that, since the stock ledger of the Kirtland bank was not available, it had contained a record of illicit transactions. That ledger finally was discovered among documents of the Chicago

Historical Society. A comment on this in an article in *BYU Studies* reads: "There are a few irregularities in the ledger, but they do not suggest dishonesty. . . . We now see that the existence of the ledger disproves the allegations of fraud or dishonesty on the part of the Church leaders in Kirtland who had allegedly destroyed the ledger to hide the evidence of their evil."[59]

It is difficult to determine at this point whether it would have been possible to avert in the case of the Kirtland bank the effects of the financial crisis. There is evidence that non-LDS enemies of the Church initiated the run on the bank that caused the suspension of redemption in coin.[60] And Truman O. Angell was convinced that "this institution would have been a financial success and a blessing to the Saints—which they needed very much—had the Gentiles who borrowed the money of the Bank fulfilled their promises."[61]

Later history of the Kirtland Temple was tied up with the changing history of the area. Most of the faithful Saints responded to the call to move to Missouri in 1838–39, but some remained. Another large group moved to Illinois in 1843 to join with the Saints there, leaving a small branch in Kirtland. A few years later apostates took over the temple, and for thirty years or so it was used for both religious and community purposes. Having been abandoned at some stage, it was subjected not only to negligence and the dilapidation produced by time but also to vandalism and destructive pilfering. There is a suggestion too (though written evidence is scanty) of further pollution of that holy house by its sometime use as a shelter for livestock, stores of hay and straw being piled in the pulpit area where the Lord himself had appeared in that glorious era of dedication and endowment.

In 1880 the Reorganized Church of Jesus Christ of Latter Day Saints gained possession of the building. That organization, which subsequently restored the building to its original condition, retains ownership today.[62]

We have left until last the culminating, transcendent events that took place in the Kirtland Temple. At an afternoon meeting there on April 3, 1836, one week following the dedication, the Twelve blessed and the First Presidency distributed the sacrament.

In the reverent spirit thus induced, the curtains that secluded the pulpits from the congregation were lowered, and in the pulpit area Joseph Smith and Oliver Cowdery knelt "in solemn and silent prayer."[63] After rising from prayer, they received the glorious visitation first of the Lord Jesus Christ, then of three other heavenly beings.

What then occurred was one of the highest moments in the life of the Prophet Joseph Smith. The veil was taken from their minds, the record says, and they saw the Lord standing upon the breastwork of the pulpit before them. Not exactly on it, for under his feet, says the record, was a paved work of pure gold.[64] One wonders—is it the case that the resurrected, glorified Christ will not again touch directly this inferior planet until he descends upon the Mount of Olives, touches that mount with his celestial foot, and thus sets in train the transformation and the earthquake that prepare the earth for the Millennium?[65] Perhaps so.

The Prophet recorded that the Savior's eyes were as a flame of fire and that his countenance shone above the brightness of the sun. His hair was white as the pure snow, and his voice was as the sound of the rushing of great waters, even the voice of Jehovah. And what did he say? He said who he was. "I am the first and the last; I am he who liveth, I am he who was slain; I am your advocate with the Father."[66] And now the phrase that must have meant more to Joseph and Oliver than any phrase up until that day: "Behold, your sins are forgiven you; you are clean before me; therefore, lift up your heads and rejoice." They did. "All who are prepared, and are sufficiently pure to abide the presence of the Savior, will see Him in the solemn assembly."[67] They had now been declared sufficiently pure.

Then came that series of statements accepting the temple by Christ himself. "Behold, I have accepted this house, and my name shall be here; and I will manifest myself to my people in mercy in this house. . . . And this is the beginning of the blessing which shall be poured out upon the heads of my people. Even so. Amen."[68]

With that promise made, the Lord having prepared the way for those who were bringing keys from former dispensations,

Joseph and Oliver as joint witnesses saw Moses. He conferred upon them the keys of the gathering of Israel and the restoration of the Ten Tribes. Then they saw Elias, who came with what is recorded as the gospel of Abraham, promising both Joseph and Oliver that through them all subsequent generations should be blessed: the same promise that had been made to Abraham thousands of years before.[69] And then, to crown it all, Elijah—declaring that the time of Malachi's prophecy about hearts of fathers and children turning to each other had arrived, and conferring the keys of the sealing power. And with all that, the warning that was at the core of the Prophet's first visit from the angel Moroni, also the promise. "By this ye may know"—now that this has happened, now that Malachi's prophecy is literally fulfilled, you may know that the coming of the Lord is nigh, even at the very doors.[70]

These visitations constitute the most sublime expression of the entire Kirtland period.

# Joseph Smith as Teacher, Speaker, and Counselor

This chapter begins with a glimpse of three principles of teaching that are discernible in practice in the School of the Prophets. Even before the completion and dedication of the Kirtland Temple, the Lord commanded that a teacher be appointed for that school, and then gave specific instructions on who should be admitted to the school, where they should meet, how they should greet each other as they entered the school, and precisely how they should conduct themselves.[1] The spirit of those counsels, I believe, should apply to every gathering of Latter-day Saints. We cannot always duplicate exactly what those in that school were taught, but as an ideal framework of the attitudes that should prevail in our classrooms, council meetings, and one-on-one discussions, those verses in section 88 of the Doctrine and Covenants seem to me universal in their worth to Latter-day Saints today.

The Saints were told that no one was to be admitted to this school "save he be clean." Clean, as the Lord put it, "from the blood of this generation."[2] That phrase troubled me for a time until I realized that it didn't simply mean forgiven of the blood shed in that generation (that was the way I first interpreted it) but it meant more still. It meant that these persons, by receiving the gospel of Jesus Christ in faith and repentance and through the ordinances, would be cleansed; that whatever they had inherited, of the human, of the sinful, of the weak, down through the centuries, would be overcome until it would be proper to say that the impurities of the past had been redeemed in the present in the personality.[3]

That is a high requirement to impose on anyone. And yet in faith those early Saints aspired to it and sought to fulfill it. Having been given that charge, they were taught the three principles which should prevail in their teaching process.

First, they were not simply to listen to one speaker. A teacher was to be appointed, said the revelation, and "let not all be spokesmen at once; but let one speak at a time, and let all listen to his sayings, that when all have spoken that all may be edified of all, and that every man may have an equal privilege."[4] A beautiful teaching principle: the need for each person present to participate, contributing his insight and experience on a given theme.

Second, before the point of teaching and participating in discussion was reached, a brotherly kinship was to be established. Once their relationship with Christ was clear and vivid, they were to make covenants with each other. For this purpose a greeting to be used was given by revelation. The president or teacher was to be first in the room, and as others arrived he was to raise his arms in the spirit of the covenant and say: "Art thou a brother or brethren? I salute you in the name of the Lord Jesus Christ, in token or remembrance of the everlasting covenant, in which covenant I receive you to fellowship, in a determination that is fixed, immovable, and unchangeable, to be your friend and brother through the grace of God in the bonds of love, to walk in all the commandments of God blameless, in thanksgiving, forever and ever. Amen."[5]

The covenant in the school, then, in part was "to be your friend." It is interesting that the earlier revelations called Joseph "my servant, Joseph." Later—presumably as he grew spiritually and became more worthy—we find the Lord speaking of him as "Joseph, my son." Finally, he spoke of the Prophet and others with him as "my friends."[6] Servant, son, friend: three beautiful relationships. Not, I take it, stages in spiritual progress so much as levels of it; for in the end, those of us who are thoroughly committed to Christ remain servants, sons or daughters, and friends. Now, then, the brethren were to covenant with each other as brethren, which sons of a common father are, and as friends. "To be your friend and brother . . . to walk in all the commandments of God blameless . . . forever and ever. Amen." And then the one being greeted would either reply "Amen"—meaning "so be it"—or repeat the precise words of the greeting. In that spirit they entered the school.

The Prophet said that "there should exist the greatest freedom and familiarity among the rulers in Zion."[7] This is glorious as an ideal. But it was that very freedom, the openness of heart and soul, the sharing of the most sacred of insights, that some took advantage of and that led to the breakdown and breakup of the School of the Prophets. For what they shared was often so intimate and so sacred that it required an immense amount of self-control to ensure that one understood it properly, or to determine the propriety of mentioning it elsewhere, or not to bandy it about outside the school, or not to take advantage of it in some way. Failure to exercise this self-control meant that the confidence engendered in the beginning was sometimes destroyed.

When that confidence prevailed in their gathering, however, those brethren had the sweetest fellowship known in our dispensation. They were brethren, and they loved each other, and in that setting—and perhaps only in that setting—the Prophet was enabled to fully share things that he otherwise felt he must not. On this point a caution is given, not to nonmembers but to the members of the Church: "That which cometh from above is sacred, and must be spoken with care, and by constraint of the Spirit; and in this there is no condemnation, and ye receive the Spirit through prayer; wherefore, without this there remaineth condemnation." Similarly the Lord says to the Church: "Let all men beware how they take my name in their lips. . . . These things remain to overcome through patience."[8]

The Prophet Joseph did not betray the sacred. His brethren did not. And only those who finally capitulated to weakness and temptation broke the bond.

The third principle is in some respects as difficult. In a word, it is concentration. At a council of high priests and elders in Kirtland, the Prophet said: "No man is capable of judging a matter, in council, unless his own heart is pure; . . . we frequently are so filled with prejudice, or have a beam in our own eye, that we are not capable of passing right decisions." Joseph continued: "In ancient days councils were conducted with such strict propriety, that no one was allowed to whisper, be weary, leave the room, or get uneasy in the least, until the voice of the Lord, by revelation, or the voice of the council by the Spirit was obtained, which has not been observed in this Church to the present time. It was understood in ancient days, that if one man could stay in council, another could; and if the president could spend his time, the members could also; but in our councils, generally, one will be uneasy, another asleep; one praying, another not; one's mind on the business of the council, and another thinking on something else."[9]

The Prophet's reference to weariness is intriguing. Not allowed to be weary! How can one prevent weariness? Notice the assumption about the strength we will have if we will truly seek the Lord—even the strength to cope with weariness. This and the other human distractions common to Church meetings are preventable. The unity the Lord promised as a presupposition of his most powerful responses to prayer comes from that time of genuine concentration. His fellow Saints said that the Prophet Joseph Smith had immense power to concentrate on the topic at hand.[10]

In spirit, at least, the above three principles can undergird our procedures whenever we seek to teach and counsel.

We turn now to some of the responses of those who heard the Prophet as a speaker, and how they attempted to describe what they heard. Let me say first that, so far as can be determined, the Prophet never read a book on the principles of "rhetoric" or "elocution." What he had been counseled to do as speaker came straight through the channel of revelation. In that mode, while he was away on a mission, he received what is now section 100 of the Doctrine and Covenants. He was counseled to "declare whatsoever thing you declare in my name, in solemnity of heart, in the spirit of meekness, in all things," and that if he would do this, "the Holy Ghost shall be shed forth in bearing record unto all things whatsoever ye shall say."[11] The Lord makes that a commandment. In this connection, Doctrine and Covenants section 84, with parallels elsewhere, contains the statement, "Treasure up in your minds continually the words of life, and it shall be given you in the very hour that portion that shall be meted unto every man."[12] The last half of that promise is widely quoted in the Church—in the very hour of our need the Lord will give us what we should speak. But this omits the governing condition, the prior clause: *if* you treasure up continually the words of life, then—and the sense of the expression is *only* if you do this—you will be given in the very hour what you should say.

Being immensely weighted with every variety of responsibility and concern, the Prophet was not able consistently to set aside long periods of time for study, though he always made the time for upreaching prayer and communion. On one occasion he arose and said, "I am not like other men. My mind is continually occupied with the business of the day, and I have to depend entirely upon the living God for every thing I say on such occasions as these."[13] Then he proceeded to deliver one of the great discourses of all time. He was "treasuring up continually," in all that that phrase implies. Therefore he was blessed with discernment to know what should be given by way of milk here and what by way of meat there.

Incidentally, the Prophet, loving, playful, and cheerful though he was, did not balk when he was inspired to rebuke or to admonish with sharpness.[14] After the rebuke, he would show forth an increase of love to the one rebuked, in accordance with Doctrine and Covenants 121:43. But he could be towering when he rebuked and it could penetrate to the very vitals.

Illustrative of this is a story still carried in the family lore of Brigham Young's descendants but, so far as I know, never recorded. It says that in a meeting the Prophet rebuked Brigham Young from his head to his feet for something he had done, or something he was supposed to have done but hadn't—the detail is unclear. And it may well have been that the Prophet was deliberately putting Brigham Young to a test. When he had finished the rebuke, everyone in the room waited for the response. Brigham Young rose to his feet. He was a strong man. He could have responded: "Now, look, haven't you read that you're not supposed to rebuke in public, but only in private?" Or, "Brother Joseph, doesn't it say something in the revelations about persuasion, and long-suffering, and gentleness and meekness?" Or, "You're dead wrong. It's not so." But he said none of the above. In a voice everyone could tell was sincere, he said simply, "Joseph, what do you want me to do?" And the story says that the Prophet burst into tears, came down from the stand, threw his arms around Brigham, and said, in effect, "Brother Brigham, you passed."[15]

As we have seen, Joseph had been taught in revelation to be humble. He had been taught to treasure up the words of life continually. In addition there was the Lord's counsel—section 50 of the Doctrine and Covenants gives it eloquent description—that without the Spirit, we can neither teach nor receive truth effectively; no matter what we know, or think we know. Literally, it is as the Savior said: "Without me ye can do nothing."[16] That may be intimidating to those of us who are proud, but it is eternally true, and Joseph knew it.

The revelation goes on to say: "Why is it that ye cannot understand and know, that he that receiveth the word by the Spirit of truth receiveth it as it is preached by the Spirit of truth? Wherefore, he that preacheth and he that receiveth understand one another, and both are edified and rejoice together."[17] One of the high privileges of teaching and serving in the kingdom is that when the Spirit is present the teacher is as blessed as, if not more so than, the student. In fact, under the Spirit every teacher himself learns. President Marion G. Romney said: "I know I was inspired tonight. I taught things I did not until then know."[18] The Prophet Joseph sought for that Spirit, and it was that, more than any other quality one can name, that gave his words convincing power.

To Hyrum, who aspired early to go into the mission field, a special revelation was given. It says, among other things, "Seek not to declare my word, but seek first to obtain my word, and then shall your tongue be loosed; then, if you desire, you shall have my

Spirit and my word, yea, the power of God unto the convincing of men."[19] There is the Lord's definition of his Spirit and his word in one phrase, "the power of God unto the convincing of men." Hyrum came to that, and so did his brother Joseph.

As regards a speaking style, Joseph warned the brethren against a kind of false or strained tone of voice that could develop in the pulpit or even in conversation.[20] It was as if he were saying that the most natural tone is also the most approved of God; the most conversational mode of speaking rather than a falsetto, or a strain, or a tense or overblown kind of eloquence.

Now to witnesses.

Brigham Young said this: "The excellency of the glory of the character of brother Joseph Smith was that he could reduce heavenly things to the understanding of the finite. When he preached to the people . . . he reduced his teachings to the capacity of every man, woman, and child, making them as plain as a well-defined pathway."[21] In that connection, speaking of Christ the Prophet said, "If He comes to a little child, he will adapt himself to the language and capacity of a little child."[22] In the preface to the Doctrine and Covenants, the Lord says, "These commandments are . . . given unto my servants in their weakness, after the manner of their language."[23] That is all we have to work with at this stage. But the Spirit can take us beyond those small chopping-blocks of meaning.

Wilford Woodruff: "I went up to the House of the Lord and heard the Prophet Joseph address the people for several hours. He had been absent from Kirtland on business for the Church. Though he had not been away half as long as Moses was in the Mount, yet many were stirred up in their hearts, and some were against him as the Israelites were against Moses; but when he arose in the power of God in the midst of them, they were put to silence, for the murmurers saw that he stood in the power of a Prophet of the Lord God."[24]

Emmeline B. Wells: "The power of God rested upon him to such a degree that on many occasions he seemed transfigured. His expression was mild and almost childlike in repose; and when addressing the people, who loved him it seemed to adoration, the glory of his countenance was beyond description. At other times the great power of his manner, more than of his voice (which was sublimely eloquent to me) seemed to shake the place on which we stood and penetrate the inmost soul of his hearers, and I am sure that then they would have laid down their lives to defend him."[25]

Mary Ann Winters: "I stood close by the Prophet while he was preaching to the Indians in the Grove by the Temple. The Holy Spirit lighted up his countenance till it glowed like a halo around him, and his words penetrated the hearts of all who heard him and the Indians looked as solemn as Eternity."[26] This is consistent with a reported occasion on which he crossed the river from Nauvoo to speak to a large group of assembled Indians about the Book of Mormon. The Indian agent, a government appointee, offered to interpret for him, but instead he began misrepresenting the Prophet's words to convey threats that the Mormons would arm themselves and drive the Indians from their land. In a miraculous manner, the Prophet understood what the man was saying. By this time the audience was becoming angry and restive, but despite the growing threat Joseph stepped boldly forward, pushed the agent aside, and began to speak to them in English. Almost immediately a calm came over the warriors and they soon released their hold on stones and other weapons, for they understood what the Prophet was saying as if he were speaking in their own tongue.[27]

Lorenzo Snow: "The Prophet Joseph Smith was not a natural orator, but his sentiments were so sublime and far-reaching that everybody was eager to hear his discourses."[28]

Isabella Horne: "I heard him relate his first vision when the Father and Son appeared to him; also his receiving the gold plates from the Angel Moroni. This recital was given in compliance with a special request of a few particular friends in the home of Sister Walton, whose house was ever open to the Saints. While he was relating the circumstances the Prophet's countenance lighted up, and so wonderful a power accompanied his words that everybody who heard them felt his influence and power, and none could doubt the truth of his narration."[29]

Alfred Cordon: "In the morning of Sunday when the weather was favorable we attended meeting ground. [That was the ground area where they were building the temple.] And with what eagerness did the people assemble to hear the words of the Prophet. One lecture from his mouth well repaid me for all my troubles and journeyings to this land, which were not a few."[30]

Angus M. Cannon: "He was one of the grandest samples of manhood that I ever saw walk or ride at the head of a legion of men. In listening to him as he has addressed the Saints his words have so affected me that I would rise upon my feet in the agitation that would take hold of my mind."[31]

Many are the testimonies of the Prophet's countenance becoming somehow alight or illumined on occasion. For example, we read in *Lydia Knight's History* of his being in Mount Pleasant, Ontario, Canada in 1833: "The Prophet commenced by relating the scenes of his early life. He told how the angel visited him, of his finding the plates, the translation of them, and gave a short account of the matter contained in the Book of Mormon. As the speaker continued his wonderful narrative, Lydia, who was listening and watching him intently, saw his face become white, and a shining glow seemed to beam from every feature." She joined the Church.[32]

There is much more we could recount on this topic, but enough has been said to show that, whatever may have been the natural gifts of the Prophet as a speaker, those who came hungering and thirsting and listened in faith felt and responded to the Spirit of God. One example is a simple discourse which changed a man's life: The Prophet was speaking on one verse of the Gospel of John.[33] "Except a man be born again," says the verse, "he cannot see the kingdom of God." Then came Nicodemus's questions. How can it be? Can a man enter the second time into his mother's womb? The Master replied, "I say unto thee, except a man be born of water and of the Spirit, he cannot enter into the kingdom of God." In his discourse the Prophet drew a distinction between *seeing* the kingdom of God and *entering* the kingdom of God; as if one must have a kind of prebirth, a kind of preliminary rebirth even to recognize that the kingdom of God is, in fact, with us, among us.

The Prophet changed the word *within*. The King James version uses that word: "The kingdom of God is *within* you."[34] In the

Joseph Smith Translation the phrase is rendered: "The kingdom of God has already come unto you"—that is, it is *among* you. (The *you* here is plural.) One has to have a rebirth even to *see* it. The scales have to fall from the eyes in a measure, by the influence of the Spirit, before a person recognizes that the Lord's kingdom is there and that he is outside of it. Once that happens, if the seed of faith is generated, he comes to the point at which he will receive it in its first principles and ordinances. Then he *enters* the kingdom of God.[35]

As a young man, Daniel Tyler heard and recorded that discourse. He became one of the great LDS patriarchs.[36]

We have said something about Joseph Smith's teaching and speaking roles. Now to the role of counselor. There is a difference between speaking, testifying, and teaching, and that setting in which soul is alone with soul. And in this again the Prophet was a master.

I have indicated that he occasionally, deliberately, knowingly, put men to a test, almost as if he could discern the spiritual growth and blessing that would ultimately result. Bishop Edwin D. Woolley was a forbear of President Spencer W. Kimball. He was a stubborn man (he himself said it)—*contrary* was the word they used in those days. It was said of him, "If he dies by drowning, look for the body upstream." Edwin D. Woolley had a store in Nauvoo, and one day the Prophet said to him, "Brother Woolley, we want all your goods for the building up of the kingdom of God," or words to that effect. Brother Woolley did as he was asked, packing his whole stock ready to be moved. Then he went to ask Joseph what he wished him to do about the goods he had received for sale on commission. Was he ready to hand all the other goods over to the Church? the Prophet asked. Brother Woolley said he was. His eyes moist, the Prophet put his hand on the other man's shoulder and said, "The Lord bless you. Put them back on the shelves."[37]

We have mentioned that Brigham Young had his tests. So did Heber C. Kimball—he was tried to the core. I believe there are those even in the Church who would say in their hearts that the test of Abraham is too much; that a loving God would not require such a thing of any man, least of all someone as faithful as Abraham. Those who have such thoughts had better think again. Modern revelation indicates at least three times that each of us who seeks eternal life must one day be tried, even as Abraham.[38] I put the question once to President Hugh B. Brown, when we were in Israel: Why was Abraham commanded to go up on that mountain (traditionally Mount Moriah in Jerusalem) and offer as a sacrifice his only hope for the promised posterity? President Brown wisely replied, "Abraham needed to learn something about Abraham."[39] By being tested, all of us will one day know how much our hearts are really set on the kingdom of God.

Heber C. Kimball's test was of that kind. A pure and humble man, at the restoration of the principle of plural marriage he was commanded—and that's the word, not counselled—to take a second wife; and to make it worse, in that soul-wrenching setting he was told he must not yet confide this to his own companion, Vilate, whom he loved with a pure love, and with whom he had shared his spiritual life since their marriage, and particularly from the time they entered the Church. At the time of his baptism a voice had spoken to him, giving him some insight into his origins, his genealogy, and also whispering of things yet future. One thing he was told by the Spirit even then was that he and his wife would never be separated.[40] Now, years later, he was being asked by a prophet to become separate in a sense—to enter plural marriage.

Filled with anxiety, Heber spent much of his nights pacing the floor. His dear Vilate begged him to tell her what was wrong, but because the Prophet had told him not to he couldn't and wouldn't. Finally, she in faith and desperate need went to her room and poured out her soul to God. "What is it, O Lord? How can I help my beloved?" And the Lord saw fit to give her a wonderful manifestation, for she saw and heard unspeakable things. She returned to her husband, her face aglow, and said, "Heber, what you kept from me the Lord has shown to me." She covenanted to honor the principle with him. Heber, who had been supplicating the Father at the same time as she had, embraced her with comparable joy.

Heber passed the test. Later the Prophet, in tears, took him and his wife Vilate upstairs in his own store and blessed them personally and sealed upon them blessings that only come to those who have come up through affliction.[41]

As a counselor, therefore, the Prophet was not merely a sentimentalist, not one who indulged the other person or tried to pat him on the back and say, "Well, it's all right," glossing over the difficulties. Instead he saw his role, a difficult one, as putting his finger on the real need.

Another example was recalled by a man named Jesse Crosby, who one day accompanied a woman on a visit to the Prophet. She felt she had been maligned unjustly by gossip. Regarding such matters, Joseph would say: "The little foxes spoil the vines — little evils do the most damage in the Church."[42] He also said, "The devil flatters us that we are very righteous, when we are feeding on the faults of others."[43] He pointed out, "The Savior has the words of eternal life" — that is, if you really want to prize words, the Savior has the words of eternal life — and "nothing else can profit us." And then in order to make the point, he added, "There is no salvation in believing an evil report against our neighbor."[44]

But this sister had been troubled, and she came and asked for redress: she wanted the Prophet now to go to the person who was the source of the story and properly take care of it. He enquired of her in some detail and then counseled her in terms something like this: "Sister, when I have heard of a story about me [and he could have said there had been many], I sit down and think about it and pray about it, and I ask myself the question, 'Did I say something or was there something about my manner to give some basis for that story to start?' And, Sister, often if I think about it long enough I realize I have done something to give that basis. And there wells up in me a forgiveness of the person who has told that story, and a resolve that I will never do that thing again."[45]

One of the great qualities of the Prophet Joseph, not always characteristic of others, is that when he was wrong he acknowledged it. The Lord rebuked him several times. Those revelations are published alongside the revelations in which he is given promises and blessings.[46] Had he been less sincere, less honest — less of a prophet — he might have tried to suppress the personal, private rebukings and let the Church believe that he'd gone along pretty well without lapsings and slippings. But he didn't. And when others found fault with him, instead of confrontation, putting all the blame on them, the spirit of his counsel to himself as to this sister was otherwise: "Look deeper, Brother, and see if maybe there is a kernel of truth in what they are saying." That, I suggest, shows wisdom.

Parley P. Pratt records a time when he was much troubled because of a severe censure from a Church leader that he felt was unjustified. He came to the Prophet and laid it on him. One of the Prophet's gifts was that he was a powerful listener—and although that phrase might seem like a contradiction in terms, it is not. There are listeners who are weak as water, not listening at all, not hearing, not interpreting from the center self. Joseph listened powerfully. And to Elder Pratt he now listened sympathetically. Then he blessed him, encouraged him, and added, "Walk such things under your feet." Meaning, of course, "It's trivial by comparison with your calling—don't let it wear you down." Elder Pratt recorded: "I was comforted, encouraged, filled with new life."[47]

Joseph may have learned that principle from the inspiration of his retranslation of the Sermon on the Mount. There are verses there that clearly have to do with forgiving, with going the second mile—some of them specially directed to the Twelve. They were told not to appeal to law, not to exact their just due, even if in fact it was just. They were told to move on—they hadn't the time to take offense at each little thing that happens in a day. They were to get on with the work of the ministry. There are those of us who seem to think that our calling is to draw a line and then spend our lives seeing that no one steps over it. Not so. Not a disciple of Christ.

And finally, again Brigham Young: He told the Prophet in the spring of 1844, "Joseph, you're laying out work for 20 years." And the Prophet replied, "You have as yet scarcely begun to work; but I will set you enough to last you during your lives, for I am going to rest."[48] Years later President Young said: "From the first time I saw the Prophet Joseph I never lost a word that came from him concerning the kingdom. . . . I was anxious to learn from Joseph and the spirit of God." He was not ascribing this knowledge and wisdom to Joseph the man; he recognized that there was a fountain to which this man had access.

To Brigham Young, the revelations of the Prophet were to be "treasured"—he would say that they were more precious than all the wealth of the world. Now Brigham Young has been criticized as a temporally-minded man, a money-minded man—even, some have said, an autocrat. Well, he had a capacity for earning and for spending, and he was a man who understood basic principles of economics. But the Prophet Joseph well knew that. He knew that when Brigham consecrated his efforts, far from that being a weakness to be blindly condemned it would be, in the hands of the Lord, a blessing. Brigham meant what he said about treasuring Joseph's words beyond all earthly wealth: "This is the key of knowledge that I have today, that I did hearken to the words of Joseph, and treasured them up in my heart, laid them away, asking my Father in the name of his Son Jesus to bring them to my mind when needed. I treasured up the things of God, and this is the key that I hold today."[49]

Brigham Young never claimed he was a great leader independent of Joseph Smith. Some have said, "Yes, Joseph was the spiritual leader, Brigham the colonizer." This is a distortion. Brigham went with Joseph on a march approximately the same length—Kirtland to Independence—as from Winter Quarters to Salt Lake City. Much of what he knew about how to command a body of men in the spirit of Israel he learned firsthand and in that laboratory with Joseph Smith.

In sum, then, Joseph Smith was, whatever his natural gifts, supernaturally blessed to teach, to speak, and to counsel. This was a major component in his unusual power. Josiah Quincy, later mayor of Boston, said to him, "You have too much power." Joseph replied, according to Quincy: "In your hands or that of any other person, so much power would, no doubt, be dangerous. I am the only man in the world whom it would be safe to trust with it." Then five words spoken as a "rich, comical aside," Quincy says: "Remember, I am a prophet!"[50]

And he was.

7

# Doctrinal Development and the Nauvoo Era

At Nauvoo in the early 1840s (the date is not certain) the Prophet Joseph Smith gave a great discourse on the temple. He said, among other things: "Now, brethren, I obligate myself to build as great a temple as ever Solomon did, if the Church will back me up." He closed by saying: "And if it should be the will of God that I might live to behold that temple completed and finished from the foundation to the top stone, I will say, 'Oh, Lord, it is enough. Let thy servant depart in peace,' which is my earnest prayer in the name of the Lord Jesus. Amen."[1]

As the months passed and the difficulties increased, apparently he came to feel by the Spirit that he would not live to see the Nauvoo Temple finished. In anticipation of that, he made several important decisions.

On May 4, 1842, he called to his side nine of the most faithful of his brethren—Hyrum Smith, Brigham Young, Heber C. Kimball, Willard Richards, Newell K. Whitney, and others—and later their wives came with them.[2]

"If it should be the will of God that I might live," he had said. Now, he continued and said in effect, "It is not the will of the Lord that I should live, and I must give you, here in this upper room, all those glorious plans and principles whereby men are entitled to the fulness of the priesthood."[3] He proceeded in an improvised and makeshift way to do so.

How did Joseph Smith know all these ordinances, and how were they transmitted to us today? The promise is recorded in section 124 of the Doctrine and Covenants, given in 1841, that the Lord would reveal to Joseph "all things pertaining to this house, and the priesthood thereof, and the place whereon it shall be built."[4] We have a further glimpse in the occasion already referred to—May 4, 1842—when a few faithful men received their endowments.[5] We have from Brigham Young this testimony, that after they had received these glorious blessings the Prophet said: "Brother Brigham, this is not arranged right. But we have done the best we could under the circumstances in which we are placed, and I wish you to take this matter in hand and organize and systematize all these ceremonies." Then, Brigham Young later said, "I did so. And each time I got something more [meaning that each time he worked on systematizing he had not only his memory and the records kept by Wilford Woodruff and others but also the light of revelation], so that when we went through the temple at Nauvoo [and without Joseph] I understood and knew how to place them there. We had our ceremonies pretty correct."[6]

Speaking of that occasion in May 1842, Joseph said: "The communications I made to this council were of things spiritual, and to be received only by the spiritual minded: and there was nothing made known to these men but what will be made known to all the Saints of the last days, so soon as they are prepared to receive, and a proper place is prepared to communicate them, even to the weakest of the Saints; therefore, let the Saints be diligent in building the Temple, and all houses which they have been, or shall hereafter be, commanded of God to build; and wait their time with patience in all meekness, faith, perseverance unto the end, knowing assuredly that all these things referred to in this Council are always governed by the principle of revelation."[7]

Other sources tell us more of what was in the heart and mind of the Prophet in this period regarding the temple. Speaking in 1835 to a group of elders about to go on missions, he had said, "You need an endowment, brethren, in order that you may be prepared and able to overcome all things."[8] Bathsheba W. Smith recorded that on one occasion the Prophet said to her, "You do not know how to pray and have your prayers answered." Then she added that when she and her husband received their endowments, they learned how to pray.[9] Mercy R. Thompson recalled that she received her temple blessings in an upper room of the Mansion House prior to the temple dedication, that the Prophet's wife, Emma, officiated, and that the Prophet said to her (Mercy Thompson), "This will bring you out of darkness into marvellous light."[10] Anticipating the inclusion of women in the temple ordinances, he told the sisters of the Relief Society, "The Church is not fully organized, in its proper order, and cannot be, until the Temple is completed."[11] More than a half-dozen of those who finally received their blessings just prior to the movement west recorded their belief that they might have been overwhelmed by the ravages of the plains and the challenges of colonization if it had not been for the blessings of the Nauvoo Temple.[12]

As for temple proxy service, Jacob Hamblin recorded: "The Prophet Joseph had told the people that the time had come which was spoken of by the Prophet Malachi, . . . the Saints must seek for the spirit of this great latter-day work [meaning the work of the temple] and that they must pray for it until they received it."[13]

Horace Cummings recorded: "Concerning the work for the dead, [Joseph] said that in the resurrection those who had been worked for would fall at the feet of those who had done their work, kiss their feet, embrace their knees and manifest the most exquisite gratitude." The Prophet added, "We do not comprehend what a blessing to them these ordinances are."[14]

One who caught the spirit of this work was Wilford Woodruff, and his journal is full of memories and details. Wilford Woodruff is the man who wrote in a journal almost every day for sixty-three years, thereby producing perhaps the most important single historical treasure we have in the Church.[15] Why did he keep the journal? Because the Prophet admonished him to. By my estimate, more than two-thirds of what we have of firsthand records of Joseph Smith's discourses and counsels to his brethren would have been lost had it not been for Wilford Woodruff's makeshift shorthand and then staying awake, often till past midnight, transcribing his notes into readable English. In that journal Brother Woodruff recorded the Prophet's announcement that the Saints could be baptized for the dead in the Mississippi River prior to the temple's completion, but that there would come a time when the Lord would accept that no longer.[16] They would have to do it in the temple. This privilege was received with great joy, and people flocked to the riverside to be baptized on behalf of departed relatives and friends.[17] Not understanding at first, they were baptized without regard to gender—men for both men and women, and women for both men and women—and without a recorder present. But with the benefit of further thought and revelation, the Prophet was able to put this right, so that things were done in order, witnessed, and properly recorded.[18]

In the Nauvoo period, the Prophet was at least able to get a roof over his own head, with the help of his brethren, and that home became the crossroads. Visitors came, some prominent, some merely curious, and some of course intent upon his destruction. William H. Walker indicated how kind the Prophet tried to be in coping with this increasing flow.[19] Josiah Quincy, later mayor of Boston, was one of those who came.[20] Another, whose diaries we haven't been equally eager to read (they were locked up in a vault for a century), was Charles Francis Adams, son of John Quincy Adams and grandson of John Adams, both United States Presidents. Charles Francis Adams was not as impressed with Joseph as was Josiah Quincy. He was full of prejudices. He was a little unhappy about having to pay a quarter to Mother Smith in order to see the Egyptian mummies upstairs in the Mansion House. Of the Prophet's claim to be able to translate some of the inscriptions, he wrote merely, "The cool impudence of this imposture amused me." He did, however, speak of the shame and injustice of the Saints' being driven and persecuted in a country whose constitution guaranteed religious freedom. But to him, the Prophet was a lightweight and a deceiver.[21] This confirmed Wilford Woodruff's comment that "the Gentiles look upon him, and he is like a bed of gold concealed from human view."[22]

In that same home there were meetings and other efforts on the Prophet's part to strengthen his brethren and further prepare them. During the winter of 1843–44, for example, he met almost daily and sometimes twice a day with all the faithful members of the Council of the Twelve. Orson Pratt finally complained, "Why do you give us no rest?" and the Prophet replied, "The Spirit urges me."[23] Erastus Snow says of that period that he learned more in a few months in council with the Prophet than he had learned in all his life before.[24] Others, Parley P. Pratt among them, tried to keep notes. In that period Joseph reviewed every restored principle, authority, and ordinance, completing it with a summary of the summary in a meeting in late March 1844 in which he said, in effect: "Brethren, I have conferred upon you now, every key and principle and power that has been bestowed upon me. Now you must round up your shoulders and bear off the kingdom or you will be damned."[25] In that same meeting the Prophet reconfirmed to the Twelve that Brigham Young, the presiding head of the Twelve (whom he had ordained thus at Quincy, Illinois, late in 1839), held the keys of the sealing power.[26] They knew it then, they knew it later, and all that has been said about other leadership intentions of the Prophet is thus superseded.

The Prophet came to love the situation at Nauvoo—the beauty of that place, the temple, and the zealous construction efforts of the Saints. As a way of trying to prevent a recurrence of what had happened in Missouri, they had their own charter, their own plan of government, their own city ordinances. They even had their own militia, the Nauvoo Legion. It was not a great crack unit of military men, but the group of several thousand was at least drilled occasionally and was trained to be able to defend the Saints' lives and homes under pressure. It was the fear of that legion, John Taylor suggested, that postponed disaster as long as it was postponed.[27] But the irony is that, having enlisted and trained up to five thousand men, many of them very young men, the Prophet himself insisted during his final days that they must stay home during the very crisis that they might have done something to resolve. He submitted in a statesman-like way when he might instead have ordered the destruction of his enemies and laid waste much of Illinois.

We read of the organization of the women during the Nauvoo period and their full involvement in all the ministrations of the temple. I have hinted earlier of the Relief Society and its strength, what great women they were, how the Prophet charged them and pleaded with them for compassion and help. He often said it was not just their duty to aid and save the poor in a temporal way, but it was ultimately their duty to save souls.[28] He said in their midst that it is the nature of woman to have largeness of soul and compassion.[29] Emma, denominated the elect lady in an early revelation, was the president.[30] The kinship she felt with those sisters and theirs for her has sometimes been obscured. It was strong. It was moving. And what they went through and how they coped with everything from breech births to the last stages of malaria will someday be known, to their eternal credit.[31]

Nauvoo also is the place where the Church established patterns which have continued to our own generation. There, for the first time, were the rudiments of a youth organization, for example, as well as the beginnings of sacrament meetings and an orderly procedure in them. In Nauvoo there was not a Sunday School per se, but often there were Sunday meetings besides sacrament meetings—prayer meetings and teaching meetings of various descriptions. The Saints were straining then as always to outdo their resources as they struggled with missionary work; and mission after mission was opened.

The Nauvoo era also was the period of a life-and-death struggle, for there were many who by that time were organized against the Church and who swore they would bring Joseph Smith and his kingdom of blockheads to naught. Joseph would say that he had suffered interminably because he claimed to be a prophet, though in fact everyone can be a prophet. His argument went roughly like this: All around me the Christian world is saying, "There are no prophets and therefore you are a false prophet." But in fact, anyone who has the testimony of Jesus has the spirit of prophecy (Revelation 19:10), and thus is a prophet. Moreover, when a man says, "If you will do so and so you will be saved, but if not, you will not be saved," is he not making a prediction about salvation and the things of God? Therefore, being a predictor he must either be a true or a false prophet. I have been given authority to say that certain things must be done in order to inherit the fulness

of salvation, and that some of the things men have claimed are re-
quirements are not. The Holy Ghost is my witness.[32]

It is ironical that men who did not believe in prophecy nevertheless predicted that the Church would fail. "Thus ends Mormonism," said a newspaper headline the morning after the
Prophet was killed. Mormonism has not ended.[33]

At the end of the Wentworth letter (written in 1842) the
Prophet wrote a paragraph which I reread in moments of discour-
agement. "No unhallowed hand can stop this work from progress-
ing; persecutions may rage, mobs may combine, armies may assemble, calumny may defame, but the truth of God will go forth
boldly, nobly, and independent, till it has penetrated every continent, visited every clime, swept every country, and sounded in
every ear, till the purposes of God shall be accomplished, and the
great Jehovah shall say the work is done."[34] Magnificent, prophetic promise!

But just as he said that, he also said that as the work of the
kingdom of God increases and expands, so the work of opposition
will increase and expand; and that the closer we come to living celestial law, the greater the opposition to be expected.[35]

Let us now focus on some gems that came from the Prophet in
this period that are not as well known as others of our scriptures,
but which were nevertheless recorded by those whom we can trust.

"Mormonism," he wrote, "is the pure doctrine of Jesus Christ;
of which I myself am not ashamed."[36] When asked what was different about Mormonism, he replied in effect, "We teach and testify of Jesus Christ."[37] To the President of the United States he
responded by emphasizing the gift of the Holy Ghost: "In our interview with the President, he interrogated us wherein we differed
in our religion from the other religions of the day. Brother Joseph
said we differed in mode of baptism, and the gift of the Holy Ghost
by the laying on of hands. We considered that all other considera-
tions were contained in the gift of the Holy Ghost."[38]

Of the Holy Ghost he said elsewhere: "If you will listen to the
first promptings you will get it right nine times out of ten."[39] He is
talking here of the impressions—elsewhere he speaks of
flashes—that come from the Spirit. All of us tend to second- and

third-guess these promptings (apparently women do it less than men). For instance, we are given a Church assignment, and an impression comes as to what to do with it. And then we begin to forget; we start to analyze and doubt. How shall we do it? Nine out of ten times "the first promptings." That was his counsel. It is wisdom.

Here are some other gems:

"No one can ever enter the celestial kingdom unless he is strictly honest."[40] That's a hard one. My own bishop has told me that when he asks individuals whether they are strictly honest, most people reply, "I try." Eventually we must do more than "try."

Another comment on honesty: "A man who has an honest heart," said the Prophet, "should rejoice."[41]

"Any man who will not fight for his wife and children is a coward."[42] Joseph Smith, the Prophet of the Lord Jesus Christ, was not a pacifist. Yes, his voice was always for peace. But read Doctrine and Covenants section 98. "It may be," he said, "that the Saints will have to beat their plows into swords, for it will not do for men to sit down patiently and see their children destroyed." The Prophet felt, and said elsewhere, that one thing uglier than war is cowardice and the refusal to stand for one's own loved ones in the breach.[43]

Speaking of gratitude he once remarked that if you will thank the Lord with all your heart every night for all the blessings of that day you will eventually find yourself exalted in the kingdom of God.[44] This is a powerful statement on the spiritual necessity of gratitude. The scripture says, "He who receiveth all things with thankfulness [notice the "all" in that: difficulties, strains, disaster, setbacks] shall be made glorious; and the things of this earth shall be added unto him, even an hundred fold, yea, more."[45] Joseph was one of the most grateful men who ever lived.

Oral tradition attributes another wise maxim to the Prophet: "Don't climb to the extreme branches of the tree, for there is danger of falling: cling close to the trunk." One translation: Avoid the vain mysteries and the discussion of them. Avoid imaginative speculation. But Joseph Smith, one must quickly add, made a distinction between the mysteries of godliness—that is, the deeper things that can only be known by revelation to the soul on the how of living a godly life—and the speculative pursuit of matters that are without profit to the soul. "I advise all to go on to perfection," he said, "and search deeper and deeper into the mysteries of Godliness."[46] The vain mysteries are those of which we know nothing and need not know anything—whether, for example, the pearly gates swing or roll, or what is the ultimate destiny of the sons of perdition. "Cling close to the trunk."

Now one of the strongest and wisest statements I have ever heard on egoism. The question was put to him, "Joseph, is the principle of self-aggrandizement wrong? Should we seek our own good?" Listen to his answer. "It is a correct principle and may be indulged upon only one rule or plan—and that is to elevate, benefit, and bless others first. If you will elevate others, the very work itself will exalt you. Upon no other plan can a man justly and permanently aggrandize himself."[47] That is another way of saying with the New Testament, "Whosoever shall lose his life for my sake and the gospel's, the same shall save it."[48] To paraphrase: He that seeketh to save his life has mere physical survival. He that is against me, or indifferent to me, will lose it. "What shall it profit a man, if he shall gain the whole world, and lose his own soul?"[49] Nothing.

Through all his Nauvoo teachings Joseph displayed a sense of mission. Lorenzo Snow reported a day when someone came and asked Joseph (it had happened hundred of times), "Who are you?" He replied, "Noah came before the flood. I have come before the fire."[50] That leads to a probing question: How much did Joseph Smith know about himself and his own calling? Clearly his knowledge grew and expanded from the initial encounters of the Sacred Grove. But what really was implicated in that tantalizing phrase picked up by enemies and friends, "You do not know me"? Or, in his turning to people on the stand (this happened at least three times in Nauvoo) and saying, "If I revealed all that has been made known to me, scarcely a man on this stand would stay with me"?[51] In another case he said, "If the Church knew all the commandments, one-half they would condemn through prejudice and ignorance."[52] To a group he once said: "Brethren, if I were to tell you all I know of the kingdom of God, I do know that you would rise up and kill me." Brigham arose and said, "Don't tell me anything that I can't bear, for I don't want to apostatize."[53]

Two things on record may help with questions about the scope of Joseph Smith's role. In a Nauvoo discourse[54] Joseph refers to the first chapter of John wherein John the Baptist was asked, "Who art thou?" He replied that he was not the Christ. "What then? Art thou Elias? Art thou that prophet [who is to come]?"[55] Joseph's critics would have thought it a stretch for him to say, "You see, there is a reference to a great prophet to come. I am he." With the discovery of the Dead Sea Scrolls and embellished traditions, sometimes fanciful, in later Judaism, it becomes apparent that two centuries before Christ a tradition taught that there were two messianic figures to come. The Messiah ben Judah, the Son of Judah, the Son of David, the Stem of Jesse, would indeed redeem. But alongside that set of prophecies and all they entailed was another set about a son of Joseph who would be a restorer of all things.[56] I said to a Harvard scholar who was famous for his New Testament skill, "What possibly could be restored?" He said, "Well, you know the phrase in the Lord's Prayer that says 'Thy kingdom come.' This was to be offered by Christians who had just received the kingdom in Jesus. But clearly the prayer presupposes that something more is to come." Then he said, "There's also that language in the Book of Acts about the 'restitution of all things.' "[57] This man is an expert on the Dead Sea Scrolls. He knows nothing of Joseph Smith (or didn't before we had our conversation). If the restorer wasn't a Joseph named Smith, the world must wait for "that prophet who is to come," who is to restore all things.[58]

We might wonder if the Prophet himself knew of these ancient patterns, if he had a glimpse that there was such a strand, down through the centuries, even between the periods of the Old and the New Testaments, when men had that word-of-mouth tradition. If so, did he recognize his own greatness in that term?

In this discourse, he speaks of seven dispensations, and says that the one Joseph led would be the last dispensation.[59] His brother Hyrum, who surely saw him as a man and as a brother, yet said earnestly, "There were prophets before, but Joseph has the spirit and power of all the prophets."[60]

Joseph knew that he had been called in this the greatest of all dispensations. And I think he knew that meant something as to his own calling, a calling that was initiated before this world was created.

That leads to the second point on which he gives us a little insight. "Every man," he said, "who has a calling to minister to the inhabitants of the world, was ordained to that very purpose in the Grand Council of heaven before this world was." And then he added, with some care and caution, "I suppose that I was ordained to this very office in that Grand Council."[61] But he didn't merely suppose. By the end, he knew.

Brigham Young, who went without bread and much else in order to hear the Prophet speak on any subject at any time, even if he was only expressing opinions—that same Brigham Young who would die with the name of Joseph on his lips—once said, in a family reunion in Nauvoo, that what Joseph had in mind in saying, "You do not know me" was essentially a matter of heritage and blood.[62] The Lord God had made covenant with Joseph who was sold into Egypt that in the last days that branch of Israel would indeed run over the wall, and God by appropriate unions of ancestors had watched over that blood until it came pure and unsullied into Joseph.[63]

Brigham Young suggested Joseph was conscious of this preordained role and how the Lord had brought it about. As to the latter, an interesting letter was written from Orson Pratt to his brother Parley P. Pratt in the 1850s that says in effect: "You will recall that Joseph had a vision in which he saw that our ancestral line [meaning the Pratt brothers] and his [meaning the Smiths] had a common ancestor a few generations back."[64] Apparently neither Parley nor Orson was able to confirm the link. The letter remained in an attic until about 1930, but then a granddaughter took it to Archibald F. Bennett, one of the outstanding genealogists of the Church, and he did the research.

He discovered that several generations back from Joseph Smith there was indeed a common ancestor named John Lathrop, and that not only was he the common ancestor of the Pratt brothers and Joseph Smith but also of other early Church leaders, including Wilford Woodruff, Oliver Cowdery, and Frederick G.

Williams. In fact one estimate concludes that one-fourth of the early Church members in America were descended from John Lathrop.[65]

The Prophet taught we would one day discover that all of us, regardless of our present guesses and researchings as to origins and family, have in our veins the cumulative blood of Israel, and whether by actual birth or by adoption into the kingdom, or both, the Almighty intends that we shall belong literally to the family of Abraham. Those of us who have mostly gentile inheritance will find that through the renovating powers of the Holy Ghost we are made, as Joseph said, literally the seed of Abraham. The visible effect of that experience, he said, may be more powerful than is the impact of the Holy Ghost on others who have more of the blood of Ephraim.[66] The kingdom is not a "closed shop." It is not a power-mongering super-race. It is an open family into which we are grafted, and through which probably most of us have a heavy genealogical debt.

Joseph was an Ephraimite. He was ordained in the Grand Council before the world was. And he was that great prophet who was to come.

# The Last Months and Martyrdom

The martyrdom of a prophet:

It is winter 1844, and the Prophet Joseph Smith is Lieutenant General of the Nauvoo Legion, mayor of the city which has become the largest and most flourishing in all of Illinois, and revelator to the Saints. But he is a man whose time is running out. To Elizabeth Rollins he had confided in the spring of 1844, "I must seal my testimony with my blood."[1] The testament is of no force, Paul said, until the death of the testator.[2] The depth of that doctrine is beyond me—why death should somehow be the full glorifying sanction of life; why blood must be shed as the price of freedom and of truth, and most of all of the witness of Christ. But so it is. Joseph taught that principle.

The brethren became anxious about his life, so often did he express the sentiment that they must carry on in his absence. Brigham Young, for one, recalled: "I heard Joseph say many a time, 'I shall not live until I am forty years of age.' "[3] At another time Brigham Young added, "Yet we all cherished hopes that that would be a false prophecy, and we should keep him for ever with us; we thought our faith would outreach it, but we were mistaken."[4]

Wilford Woodruff, who conversed with the Prophet just after April Conference 1844, recalled that he later sent ten of the Twelve

East on a mission, and that the Prophet seemed to linger in saying goodbye to him. Then, looking him through and through, he said, "Brother Woodruff, I want you to go, and if you do not, you will die." And he looked "unspeakably sorrowful, as if weighed down by a foreboding of something dreadful."[5]

On the other hand, because he had so often escaped the vilifyings and the attacks of his enemies, some believed that he was invincible. In one sermon he said, in response, "Some have supposed that Brother Joseph could not die; but this is a mistake." He added, "Having now accomplished [my work], I have not at present any lease of my life. I am as liable to die as other men."[6]

During that last winter he manifested four dominant anxieties and did all in his power to relieve them, as he had been commanded. The first anxiety related to the temple. He yearned for it to be finished. For example, he with Hyrum went from house to house in Nauvoo in the role, we would say now, of home teachers, and recommitted the Saints to give of time and means to the speedy erection of that building.[7] He himself gave sermons and so did Hyrum.[8] Hyrum said, "Great things are to grow out of that house."[9] Joseph did some of the physical work himself, quarrying rock with his bare hands.[10] Often he would ride out on his horse, Old Charlie, sometimes accompanied by his dog, Major, ride up on the hill, that commanding eminence, to the temple site, longing and praying that the Saints would be able to complete it and receive the blessings to be given therein before they were driven and scattered. For he anticipated and prophesied that they would be driven and scattered.[11]

Joseph's anxiety about the temple was compounded by his anxiety concerning the records of the Church, that they be kept, preserved, and accurately transmitted. That was the responsibility of several of his scribes.[12] Six men were working around the clock to bring the history up to date. One of them was Willard Richards, a loyal man who often burned candles until midnight, writing with his quill pen. Joseph had said, after a dream, "I told Phelps a dream that the history must go ahead before anything else."[13] To several others he spoke of the necessity of accurate record-keeping, and he lamented in a priesthood meeting with "deep sorrow" that the

Church had not kept adequate minutes. He intimated that this was a matter that could offend the Lord, since he had given inspiration which they had not prized enough to record. Then Joseph said, "Here let me prophesy. The time will come when, if you neglect to do this thing, you will fall by the hands of unrighteous men."[14]

One might ask, Was it all that important? And one can quickly answer: If all of the Twelve then in Nauvoo had promptly recorded the meeting in which Joseph rolled off the responsibility from his shoulders upon them and charged them, in what he called his last charge, to go forward in building the kingdom, any claim that he intended someone else to succeed to the Presidency of the Church would be completely refuted by contemporary documents. But only one of the Twelve, Orson Hyde, recorded that meeting at the time.[15] Most of those present didn't say much about it until several years later.[16] Hence, although the charge that this meeting was a convenient afterthought is a false one, as a Church we would have been invulnerable on this point if proper records had been kept. They would have refuted any possible claim that Joseph did not want the President of the Twelve to succeed him.[17]

Crucial? Yes.

In addition to the anxiety about records, he had a concern to teach in summary all that had theretofore been made known and to make sure that the brethren understood it. To that end he spent much of every day for three months with the Twelve, with others of the Church leaders, and also often in counsel with husbands and wives, sharing, summarizing, reiterating restored truth and ordinances. "You give us no rest," Orson Pratt said. "The Spirit urges me," the Prophet replied.[18] Wilford Woodruff said: "It was not merely a few hours . . . but he spent day after day, week after week, and month after month, teaching [the Twelve] and a few others the things of the kingdom of God."[19] As the record shows, even though the temple was not complete he administered the higher ordinances of the temple to certain of the more faithful and true. Thus we know of sixty to seventy couples who received temple blessings in the upper room over his store, before the Nauvoo Temple was completed.[20] By now construction was far along. The temple was, as some said, "up to the square," and the baptismal font then had been dedicated and was in use for baptisms for the dead.[21]

To summarize thus far: temple anxiety, record anxiety, teaching anxiety.

Finally there was the Prophet's major concern—that the Saints understand his role and be willing to do what in an extremity they might be required to do.[22] Strangely, throughout the days of the last of May and early June 1844 many who were associated with the Prophet exhibited unusual optimism. Among these was his brother Hyrum, who seemed to feel, even down to the time that they were in jail in Carthage, that everything would work out, that this was just one more of the many crises from which they had always emerged. In radical contrast the Prophet had for some time had all kinds of ominous presentiments.[23]

Now we reach the crisis moment, the tinder box and the trigger. In the Nauvoo period some people's attitudes were bitter. They joined in league with the underworld. At this time Nauvoo was the largest city in Illinois, hence counterfeiters, blacklegs, bootleggers, slave traders, gamblers, and every other disreputable type of person found their way there, trying to exploit the possibilities for dishonest profits, trying to gull recent and sometimes naive converts who had come from far and near. As you walked the streets of Nauvoo it was difficult to know who were the Saints and who weren't. Because of that underworld, but worse still because of apostates living there who now hated the Church, the Prophet's life was placed in jeopardy.[24]

William Law had first wept at the Prophet's announcement of the principle of plural marriage, and with his arms around Joseph's neck had pleaded that he not teach it. His son Richard, who said this took place about 1842 and who was present at the time, later related the incident to Joseph W. McMurrin, who summarized his remarks as follows: "William Law, with his arms around the neck of the Prophet, was pleading with him to withdraw the doctrine of plural marriage, which he had at that time commenced to teach to some of the brethren, Mr. Law predicting that if Joseph would abandon the doctrine, 'Mormonism' would, in fifty or one hundred years, dominate the Christian world. Mr. Law pleaded for this . . . with tears streaming from his eyes. The Prophet was also in tears, but he informed the gentleman that he could not withdraw the doctrine, for God had commanded him to teach it, and condemnation would come upon him if he was not obedient to the commandment."[25] In conversation with others of the brethren Joseph said the Lord had told him that keys would be turned against him if he did not obey the commandment. How early did he know that plural marriage would be restored? At least as early as 1832.[26] By 1842, ten years later, he had introduced it. (Of that principle, Joseph told the brethren, "I shall die for it."[27]) Over that William Law became bitter, and soon he was excommunicated.[28] Then Law attempted to organize his own church and began to fight back.[29] He and his brother, Wilson, Chauncey and Francis Higbee, and Robert and Charles Foster were the sextet responsible for the publication on June 7, 1844, of the first and only issue of the *Nauvoo Expositor*.

Written in the most intemperate language, the *Expositor* vilified the Prophet and attacked the Nauvoo Charter, which had been a protection to the Saints that they had not had in Missouri. Some examples are: "How shall he, who has drunk of the poisonous draft, teach virtue? . . . We are earnestly seeking to explode the vicious principles of Joseph Smith and those who practice the same abominations and whoredoms." Joseph Smith is "one of the blackest and basest scoundrels that has appeared upon the stage of human existence since the days of Nero and Caligula," and his followers are "heaven-daring, hell-deserving, God-forsaken villains." The paper attacked the "pretended" authority of the Nauvoo Charter as "unjust, illegal, and unconstitutional."[30]

Concerned at this threat to their liberties and their lives, the citizens were filled with indignation. The city council met. According to their understanding of law, they decided that the *Expositor* was, by their own charter, a public nuisance, and that they had the authority not only to confiscate any remaining copies of the paper but also to destroy the press.[31] Some students of law today would argue that they were perfectly within the law of the times; that there were precedents for it, and that the way they did it was indeed legal. (That was more than could be said of the 1833 mob action against the Saints in Missouri, well remembered by many Nauvoo citizens, when the printing press was pushed out of the second-story window, hundreds of printed copies of revelations were destroyed, the family with its sick child was evicted, the building was reduced to a heap of ruins, and two brethren were tarred and feathered.) But both friends and enemies of the Prophet now agree that the act, legal or not, was unwise and inflammatory and was the major immediate factor that culminated in the Prophet's death.[32]

George Laub recorded the following: "Brother Joseph called a meeting at his own house and told us that God showed to him in an open vision in daylight [meaning that this was not something he had just conjured up in dreams of the night] that if he did not destroy that printing press that it would cause the blood of the Saints to flow in the streets and by this was that evil destroyed."[33] Speaking of those who returned to report that they had destroyed the press and other materials, as ordered by the city council, Joseph recorded: "I . . . told them they had done right and that not a hair of their heads should be hurt for it."[34] No doubt, not all believed this. He did not add then, which he could have, that although he had by that act preserved the Saints' lives for a time, he had done so at the cost of his own. Even before the decision was made, the apostates had provided for it in their hearts. Francis Higbee is said to have remarked on June 10 while the city council was in session: "If they lay their hands upon it [the printing press] or break it, they may date their downfall from that very hour, and in ten days, there will not be a Mormon left in Nauvoo."[35] They threatened much more than they ever did. Among their threats were that there wouldn't be a stone left on the temple, that they would burn all of Nauvoo, that there would not be one Smith left in the state, and that the Mormons would be killed or driven.[36]

This was indeed the crisis. Tried on charges rising out of the *Expositor* case, the Prophet was twice acquitted, as were those charged with him—city council members mainly.[37] Because Joseph had avoided a hearing in Carthage, where his life would be forfeit, his enemies were not satisfied. Eventually Thomas Ford, the governor of Illinois, pronounced himself unsatisfied with those legal procedures and insisted that the Prophet go to be tried in the very hotbed of the cruelest opposition in the state, Carthage.[38] Why? Ford mentioned it in his letter: to placate the masses.[39] But after they had surrendered themselves at Carthage, the governor pledging to protect them, Joseph and Hyrum were charged with treason, and bail was set for Joseph and Hyrum and the thirteen other defendants at $7,500, for which the fifteen men plus several other brethren were able to give surety.[40] When their enemies thus found they could not get them in jail legally, they found another way, and the Smith brothers were illegally put in jail.[41]

May I now back up to some preparatory events in the Prophet's own inner life. In the King Follett discourse (April 1844) he had spoken of the great secret, the great and glorious truth, both that God himself has *become* what he is and that man, who is in the image of God, may become like him. It would help us with those to whom this seems to be blasphemy if we worded it more carefully than we usually do, if we said not "we believe that God is like a man," but rather, "God is like Christ." No genuine Christian could be offended at that statement. But we must go on to say "and as are God and his Christ, so man may be."[42] That too has offended many. The King Follett discourse, though we have published it more than any of the Prophet's public utterances, still occasions some difficulty.

At the end of that discourse, he made the now classic statement: "You don't know me; you never knew my heart. No man knows my history. I cannot tell it; I shall never undertake it."[43] The history of the Church he wrote as he was involved in it, but much of the biography of his inner world he kept locked within. At the end of the speech he said: "When I am called by the trump of the archangel and weighed in the balance, you will all know me then. I add no more. God bless you all. Amen."[44]

Many were saying then, as they had in Kirtland and before, that here was a fallen prophet.[45] Occasionally, with a twinge of humor, he would say, "Well, I had rather be a fallen true prophet than a false prophet."[46]

In the conspiracy to take his life in which the Laws were involved, two young men had been invited to the secret meetings— Dennison L. Harris and Robert Scott. They consulted with the

Prophet. He asked them to go and observe. At the risk of their lives they attended these meetings and reported back what they had heard. Prior to the last meeting they reported their expectation that at that meeting everyone present would be asked to come forward and take an oath to be willing to take the life of Joseph Smith.[47]

The Prophet wept. Now he knew by natural means as well as by his presentiments what was happening. The young men heroically attended the meeting as he suggested, and narrowly escaped with their lives when they were put under pressure to take the oath.

Joseph can be described properly, as he was by B. H. Roberts, as a man who "lived his life in crescendo." There was no diminuendo in his life, but always increase.[48] He gave the last of his discourses in the Grove. After the Laws had prophesied that he would never speak from the stand again, and though the rain at the end shortened his talk, he delivered a masterful discourse on the testimony he had borne from the beginning that the Father, the Son, and the Holy Ghost are three separate personages.[49] In the final moment of his discourse he said, "Brethren and sisters, love one another; love one another and be merciful to your enemies." Lucy M. Smith later recalled, "He repeated these words in a very emphatic tone of voice with a loud amen."[50] After that address he said he yearned to preach once more. His subject would have been a passage out of John's Revelation pertaining to our becoming kings and priests.[51]

Then came the moment, the discourse before the Legion. Some of our historians have candidly observed that this was Joseph Smith as a man; this wasn't really the Prophet, it was humanity coming out. He stood "on the top of the frame of a building," the frame of the unfinished Nauvoo House.[52] Before the group, many of them in uniform, he said, as he had twice before, that now the moment had been reached when "I will never tamely submit to the dominion of cursed mobocracy."[53] He summarized how he had been driven as a roe on the mountains[54] all his life, that his enemies had given him no rest. When they took away his own rights, he said, he would submit. When they took away the rights of the Saints, he would fight for them. Now he unsheathed his sword and said, "I call God and angels to witness [what I have said]."[55]

If his language on this occasion seems inflammatory, one should read the journals of some of those who were present. They speak of the Prophet as "calm and deliberate."[56] They speak of him as concerned in love for his brethren.[57] He did cry out at one point, "Will you stand by me to the death?" and thousands shouted "Aye!" He responded, "It is well." Then in a wave of assurance of his own soul he said, "This people shall have their legal rights, and be protected from mob violence, or my blood shall be spilt upon the ground like water." And again, "I am willing to sacrifice my life for your preservation."[58]

If we can understand what was inside of him in love for his brethren, we will understand why his soul was wounded to the core when men came across the river at Montrose and accused him of cowardice—said that, despite his words about standing up for them, now that trouble had come he was the first one to run.[59] That's when he replied, "If my life is of no value to my friends it is of none to myself." That was when the resolve was made to return. He had had light in his decision to leave—"It is clear to my mind what to do."[60] We can certainly say that the death of the Prophet was brought on by his enemies. Perhaps we must also say that it was brought on by some of his friends.

After all that the Saints had received from Joseph, there were some who at that stage could not believe him when he said, "All they want is Hyrum and myself. . . . They will come here and search for us. Let them search; they will not harm you . . . not even a hair of your head. We will cross the river tonight, and go away to the West."[61] But the pot was boiling. Reports were coming in every hour telling of increasing numbers of men who had come from Missouri to join the Illinois mobs; the mobs that were being gathered, the cannons they had available, the threats they were making.[62] In the midst of that flood of evidence, Joseph's statement, "You will be safe," could not be believed. More than a hundred, Vilate Kimball wrote, had left Nauvoo. Seeing them go, the Prophet said, "Look at the cowards." Now he himself was called a coward.[63] And against the light, he came back. "The light he had was toward the mountains."[64]

Porter Rockwell, when asked what he thought should be done, replied to the Prophet in a nineteenth-century phrase—"As you make your bed, I will lie with you." Said Joseph, "Hyrum, you are the oldest, what shall we do?" Hyrum answered, "Let us go back and give ourselves up." The Prophet, probably thinking of the governor's stern, uncompromising letter, said, "If you go back I will go with you, but we shall be butchered." "No, no," said Hyrum, "let us go back and put our trust in God, and we shall not be harmed."[65]

John Murdock, who watched them row back across the river that day, later said that he felt something in the air; that there was something threatening about this situation.[66] Hyrum's son, Joseph, felt it, and could never quite speak of it for the rest of his life without weeping. Mercy R. Thompson, watching from a chamber window, felt "sorrowful forebodings."[67] The two men's wives, Emma Smith and Mary Fielding Smith, were not quite so much concerned, because so often their husbands had come back from threatening circumstances, and they, of course, did all they could to soothe them. The Prophet would later write a letter to Emma from the jail. It said in part: "It is the duty of all men to protect their lives and the lives of the household, whenever necessity requires." He wrote, "Should the last extreme arrive," then didn't finish the sentence.[68]

Having recrossed the river to Nauvoo that last Sunday, June 23, Joseph sent a letter to the governor in Carthage promising to be there the next day. To meet the governor's deadline they would have to leave very early—a 6:00 a.m. departure at the latest, and they had had no sleep for two nights.

There are little moments in those last hours that are significant and poignantly memorable. I mention only a few.

After the two brothers returned to surrender state arms as ordered by the governor, Leonora Taylor was in the Smith home when the Prophet went again to say goodbye. He pleaded with Emma on that occasion to go with him, even though she did not want to risk getting the ague, chills, and fevers. She was also expecting a child (four months pregnant) and not feeling well. He begged her to come anyway. She said no. And as he turned away, he said, "Well, if they don't hang me I don't care how they kill me."[69]

It seems likely that Willard Richards overheard that statement and that that is why, in the last moments, he offered—and he meant it—to be hanged in the Prophet's stead. The Prophet's statement also tells us that he hadn't yet been made to know exactly how he would die. There had been threats, one of them published in the newspaper, that his enemies would, as the letter said, "make catfish meat of him."[70] How ruthless some of these men were! They did it with slaves. They encouraged black men to run away from their masters, and they would sell them and pocket the money; then have them run away again, and sell them and pocket the money. They would tell the slave that after the third time, when, as they said, he was "hot," they would share the money and he would be free. Instead of that they killed him, and cut him up and threw him in the Mississippi. That was making catfish meat of a man.[71]

There was also the problem of a reward offered by the Missourians. They had placed a price on his head—they would pay a thousand dollars for his delivery, as with John the Baptist, on a platter.[72]

So he did not know how he would end his life, but he did not relish—who among us would have?—the thought of hanging.

There was a moment with Daniel H. Wells, not yet a member of the Church, who was on a sickbed. The Prophet, not feeling well himself, stopped to see him. "Squire Wells, I wish you to cherish my memory, and not think me the worst man in the world either."[73] Daniel H. Wells had to give up his family in order to join the Church later.[74] He could never speak of that last encounter with Joseph without deep feeling, and he became one of our great ones.

Mary Ellen Kimball overheard the Prophet say, as the group stopped to ask for a drink of water on the way to Carthage that morning, "Brother Rosenkranz, if I never see you again, or if I never come back, remember that I love you." She felt that to her soul, and fled and wept on her bed.[75]

And then there was the pause the group made at the temple, where the Prophet lovingly surveyed that building, the city, the landscape, and then said: "This is the loveliest place and the best people under the heavens; little do they know the trials that await them."[76]

On the road to Carthage the Prophet made some revelatory expressions that are not part of the official history. Isaac Haight recorded that at one point Joseph was so weighed down that he turned to Hyrum and said, "Brother Hyrum, let us go back to Nauvoo, and all die together."[77] Hyrum urged him on. When they were several miles out from Nauvoo he instructed—and that's the only way he could get them to do so—that many who had ridden that far with him turn around and go back. John Butler recorded: "We were all willing to live or die with them. Brother Joseph spoke to us all and told us that he was like a lamb led to the slaughter. He also spoke to Brother Hyrum and wished him to return home with us. We begged him to let us stay with him and die with him, if necessary, but he said, no, we were to return to our home, and Brother Hyrum said that he would stay with Brother Joseph. For my part, I felt that something great was going to transpire. He blessed us and told us to go. We bade them farewell, and started. We had twenty miles to ride, and we went the whole distance without uttering one word. All were dumb and still, and all felt the Spirit, as I did myself. I cannot express my feelings at that time, for they overpowered me." He added, "As I turned and as we rode away I felt as I suppose the ancient disciples of Christ felt when he said, 'I must be crucified.' "[78]

And then the third expression. They stopped at the Fellows' farm after being met by a menacing group on horseback from Carthage, and Joseph went in and countersigned Governor Ford's order for the surrender of all state arms in possession of the Nauvoo Legion. "I am not afraid to die," he said.[79] In the jail the day before his death he said to his brethren: "I have had a good deal of anxiety about my safety since I left Nauvoo, which I never had before when I was under arrest. I could not help those feelings, and they have depressed me."[80]

Once Joseph and Hyrum had been jailed, many legal efforts were made in their behalf. None of these availed. Dan Jones went and personally talked to the governor, reporting the threats to the Prophet's life that he had heard uttered in various groups of men now in Carthage. The governor merely said, "You are unnecessarily alarmed for the safety of your friends, sir, the people are not that cruel."[81] A non-Mormon, Dr. Southwick, claimed that only two days before this a meeting was held that included a representative of every one of the United States. The subject was the political campaign, for Joseph Smith and Sidney Rigdon had been named respectively as candidates for the Presidency and Vice-Presidency of the United States. There were reasons for this candidacy, one of them being that it enabled five hundred men from Nauvoo to dramatize and teach the gospel in a way they could not otherwise do. Joseph did not, of course, expect to be elected. But now enough support was being generated, and was showing up in the Eastern newspapers, that men in the meeting meant to stop the political career of Joseph Smith. The Missourians present said, in effect, "If you want us to do the job, we'll do it." And the others said, "If Illinois and Missouri would join together and kill him, they would not be brought to justice for it. If you don't stop him this time, if he isn't elected this time, he will, or likely may, next time."[82] So in this struggle there were political motives as well as others.

The governor was surrounded by mobocrats, and the Saints' efforts with him failed. John Taylor, a man of great character and spine, saw the situation, was indignant, and said, "Brother Joseph, if you will permit it, and say the word, I will have you out of this prison in five hours, if the jail has to come down to do it." He planned to go to Nauvoo and raise a sufficient force. But "Brother Joseph refused."[83] Stephen Markham offered to change clothes with the Prophet, to make a switch—the Prophet could then get away on his horse and all would be well. The Prophet turned that down.[84] James W. Woods was assigned to go to Jesse Thomas, one of the circuit judges in Illinois, who had assured the Prophet that if he would send responsible Mormons to each community and explain the actions of recent days the citizens would be pacified. Woods was asked to check further into this. He found that hope too to be false, for Thomas and others said, in his presence, "Don't you think it's better for two or more men to die than for a whole neighborhood to be in an uproar?"[85] Two or three of the Prophet's non-Mormon friends, one of them a sea captain and one a dentist, were summoned to testify in his behalf. All of them tried, none of them was successful.[86]

After all these efforts, the only real thing the Prophet had between him and the final scene was a pistol which Cyrus Wheelock had brought him. When Hyrum said, "I hate to use such things or to see them used," the Prophet replied, "So do I, but we may have to, to defend ourselves."[87]

Many anti-Mormon tracts have said that it certainly is no example to the Christian world that a man should be called a martyr for Christ if he used a gun in his last hour. They do not know either the background or the sequel. The background, in a word, is that the Prophet had promised those brethren in the name of the Lord that he would defend them even if it meant giving up his life.[88] Had he been all alone in the Carthage Jail, the story might be different, but he was not. He was there with two members of the Twelve, John Taylor and Willard Richards—Willard Richards weighing over three hundred pounds, the largest target (and the only one who would not be injured)— and with his brother Hyrum. He did defend them as he had promised. In fact, we now know from the records that the first man up the stairs that day, anxious and eager, was met by a fist and rolled back down. That fist was Joseph Smith's.[89]

Inside the room they had nothing to defend themselves with except two pistols, plus two walking sticks which they used in an effort to divert the rifles. Some of the balls went off in the ceiling. When Jacob Hamblin and James W. Woods visited the room shortly after the martyrdom they counted the pockmarks of the balls that were shot through the door or doorway. There were thirty-six.[90] According to Willard Richards, all that shooting occurred in less than two minutes.[91] Both Hyrum and Joseph received five balls; John Taylor, four. It was a volley, an explosive volley.

The previous night, the Prophet had had some private conversations. We know that he had borne to the guards his testimony of the Book of Mormon and the Restoration, and later his last testimony to the brethren present.[92] No doubt it was the equivalent of what David Osborne had heard him say in 1837: "The Book of Mormon is true, just what it purports to be, and for this testimony I expect to give an account in the day of judgment."[93] We know also that earlier he had pleaded three times with Hyrum for Hyrum to leave him and go back. Hyrum could only say, "Joseph, I can't leave you."[94] Hyrum, it turned out, was the first to be killed.

How did the Prophet make the decision to leave that room, or to try to leave it, through the window? Films depict Joseph falling off balance out through a large glass plate window. There is no such window. This was a jail. Even the upstairs had walls as thick as two feet. The window was small, and Joseph was a large man, and for him to get through it required considerable effort. Willard Richards used the strangest adverb in his whole account when he said that after emptying the pistol (which misfired a couple of times) the Prophet *calmly* turned from the door, dropped the pistol, and went to the window.[95] Calmly? It is difficult to understand how anybody could have heard the words in such a fracas, but one man, outside the jail, claimed he heard the Prophet cry, "Oh Lord, what shall I do?"[96] How fast can a man's mind work in such circumstances? What was going through his? It was certain death at the door, that was clear. It was certain death at the window, because balls were coming through it, and John Taylor had just been blasted under the bed, writhing in pain with four wounds. Yet Joseph decided to get out—hoping, Willard Richards believed, that it might save the lives of his brethren.[97]

Whether that was his intent or not, he was hit from behind—twice, maybe three times—but managed anyway to pull himself up and out, and then fell from the window. "He's leaped the window!" someone shouted, and those on the landing rushed downstairs and outside.[98] "Shoot him, — — —him, shoot him!" said Levi Williams, and they shot several times more.[99] One account says that the Prophet died with a smile.[100] Perhaps he was conscious long enough to know that the promise he had made to Willard Richards had been fulfilled: "Willard . . . you will stand where the balls will fly around you like hail and men will fall dead by your side, and . . . there never shall a ball injure you."[101] Perhaps he knew that John Taylor would become the third prophet, seer, and revelator. Elder Taylor would live long enough to write a hymn, "Oh, Give Me Back My Prophet Dear,"[102] and would himself be twice "martyred," in a measure dying once at Carthage and recovering, and then dying again in exile because he would not compromise the gospel of Jesus Christ.

We return to the prophetic words of that last hymn, "A Poor Wayfaring Man of Grief." It was, in the late days of Nauvoo, the Prophet's favorite, and it was the last music he heard on earth. The final two lines are:

These deeds shall thy memorial be;
Fear not, thou didst them unto me.

For a time the Saints could not be comforted. The mourning, the black miasmic depression that descended upon Nauvoo was overwhelming. When Mary Fielding Smith, Hyrum's wife, after midnight heard the high-pitched voice of Porter Rockwell, riding on a sweaty horse, shouting, "They've killed them! they've killed Joseph and Hyrum!" she screamed. And young Joseph wept. Soon all Nauvoo knew. Some felt bitter and wanted vengeance. Some who held command positions in the Nauvoo Legion went immediately and asked that they be marshaled. But the leaders had been told by the Prophet to stay home. That was that.

Letters came to Nauvoo from both Willard Richards and John Taylor. To reassure John Taylor's family, Elder Richards wrote, "Taylor's wounded, not very badly."[103] And peace prevailed in spite of the anguish. Many of the brethren absent on missions felt forebodings that day, even at the hour of the martyrdom. Only seven days previously the Prophet had sent letters to all the Twelve asking them to return to Nauvoo immediately.[104] So it was that the returning Parley P. Pratt walked depressed across the plains of Illinois until he could hardly endure it. Finally he knelt and prayed for comfort; and then it was made known to him that the newspaper headlines he had seen in Chicago told the truth, that Joseph and Hyrum had in fact given their lives for the Lord's cause, and that he was to go back rapidly to Nauvoo and tell the Saints to do nothing until the Twelve had reassembled.[105]

Despite the provocation, then, peace and not war came in the aftermath of the Prophet's death. With their Nauvoo Legion the Saints had power to win in any skirmish had they so chosen. But they who had been stereotyped as warlike and bitter and hostile and filled with vengeance demonstrated that they were not any of those. They were peaceful.[106]

And now by way of testimony.

I stood years ago with a Church History group outside the walls of the jail in Carthage. It was a dark day, with lowering clouds and some rain. Standing there we were taught in an inspired way the details of the Prophet's last days.

The Spirit that came upon me there, I pray, will never be obliterated. I can summarize it by saying that the spirit that testifies to the souls of men that Jesus the Christ is the Son of God and that he gave his life willingly for the redemption of mankind is the same spirit that bears witness to the receptive soul that Joseph Smith was a prophet of Jesus Christ. One cannot truly say he knows the one thing and deny the other. No man can come to a testimony of the prophetic mantle of the Prophet Joseph Smith without knowing that Jesus is the Christ, the Messiah, the Anointed One. And no man can have a testimony that Christ is the divine Savior and Lord without knowing, when he hears Joseph's name and knows even a little of his life, that Christ had a prophet named Joseph Smith.

In bearing that testimony I add to it the witness that we too, somehow, someday, must reach the point at which we hold our physical life cheap, or our eternal life dear, even to the point of being willing to lay our life down in the image and pattern of the Lord Jesus Christ. "Blessed are ye," said the Lord to the Prophet early on, "even if they do unto you even as they have done unto me, . . . for you shall dwell with me in glory."[107] In 1843 the Prophet recorded the Lord's words addressed to him: "I seal upon you your exaltation, and prepare a throne for you in the kingdom of my Father, with Abraham your father."[108] In that same revelation the Lord said: "Let no one, therefore, set on my servant Joseph, . . . for he shall do the sacrifice which I require at his hands."[109]

Like many of the prophets of ancient times, the prophet of the last dispensation was martyred for the Lord's cause. "Many have marveled because of his death," the Lord told Brigham Young, "but it was needful that he should seal his testimony with his blood, that he might be honored and the wicked might be condemned."[110]

If we do not know them now, each of us will at some time come to know these twin truths: Jesus is the Christ, and Joseph is his Prophet. I bear this witness in the name of Jesus Christ. Amen.

# Author's Note on Sources

The book *Teachings of the Prophet Joseph Smith*, compiled by Joseph Fielding Smith, has long been a convenient source of doctrinal teachings of Joseph Smith contained in *History of The Church of Jesus Christ of Latter-day Saints* and other early Church publications. For the life and teachings of Joseph Smith newer tools also are now available to the casual reader as well as to the analytic student. Every document written in Joseph Smith's own hand is now collected in *The Personal Writings of Joseph Smith*, edited by Dean C. Jessee. All the Prophet's Nauvoo discourses, in their original form as recorded, have been gathered and interrelated in *The Words of Joseph Smith*, edited by Andrew F. Ehat and Lyndon W. Cook. Every doctrinal statement of the Prophet contained in the four books named above has been included, along with its immediate text, in *Concordance of Doctrinal Statements of Joseph Smith*, edited by Truman G. Madsen. Digests of three thousand diaries and journals of early Mormons, many of whom knew Joseph Smith, have been annotated in Davis Bitton's *Guide to Mormon Diaries and Autobiographies*. The new LDS edition of the Bible presents the most important changes in the Joseph Smith Translation of the scriptures, with useful footnotes and a comprehensive Topical Index.

The sources listed above, as well as many others both published and unpublished, have been used with appreciation by the author in writing this book. Punctuation and spelling have been modernized as necessary in quotations included. Publication or location details on sources cited are included in the bibliography.

# Abbreviations

The abbreviations listed below have been used to simplify references in the notes and sources that follow.

BYU Studies — *Brigham Young University Studies*

CHC — B. H. Roberts, *A Comprehensive History of The Church of Jesus Christ of Latter-day Saints*, 6 vols.

HC — Joseph Smith, *History of The Church of Jesus Christ of Latter-day Saints*, 7 vols.

IE — *The Improvement Era*

JD — *Journal of Discourses*, 26 vols.

JI — *The Juvenile Instructor*

Journal History — Journal History of The Church of Jesus Christ of Latter-day Saints

JST — Joseph Smith Translation of the Holy Bible, entries contained in the Holy Bible published by The Church of Jesus Christ of Latter-day Saints, 1979, or The Holy Scriptures, Inspired Version, published by The Reorganized Church of Jesus Christ of Latter Day Saints

MA — *Latter Day Saints' Messenger and Advocate*

MS — *The Latter-day Saints' Millennial Star*

TPJS — Joseph Smith, *Teachings of the Prophet Joseph Smith*

TS — *Times and Seasons*

WJS — Joseph Smith, *The Words of Joseph Smith*

Writings — Joseph Smith, *The Personal Writings of Joseph Smith*

YWJ — *Young Woman's Journal*

# Notes and Sources

## Introduction

1. *TPJS*, p. 366.
2. D&C 136:38.

## Chapter 1. The First Vision and Its Aftermath

1. Published under this title as a pamphlet in 1966 by Deseret Book Co.

2. *BYU Studies* 9 (Spring 1969): 278–81, 284–85, 287–93, 296. All four of the Prophet's written recitals of the First Vision along with contemporary accounts given by others can be found in Backman, *Joseph Smith's First Vision*, pp. 151–81.

3. See, for example, Lyon, "How Authentic Are Mormon Historic Sites in Vermont and New York?" pp. 341–50; Jessee, "The Early Accounts of Joseph Smith's First Vision," pp. 275-94; and Anderson, "Circumstantial Confirmation of the First Vision Through Reminiscences," pp. 373–404.

4. The 1832 account provides the most extended passage on the influence of the vaulted heavens on Joseph's convictions concerning God. See Backman, *First Vision*, pp. 156–57.

5. "This was a grief to my Soul," he said in 1832. Further, his reflections on the heavens and his searching the scriptures led him to become more conscious of his own sins and he felt to mourn for them. See Backman, *First Vision*, p. 156.

6. See Backman, *First Vision*, p. 163. He says that "it never entered into [his] *heart*" that the churches were all in error, but it may have entered his head. In his youth he leaned toward Methodism, and his mother was a Presbyterian Seeker. Yet he said in 1838, describing his earlier dilemma, that he asked himself, "Are they all wrong together?" (Backman, *First Vision*, p. 162.) But even after his first vision he never said that all the churches were *all* wrong. "Have the Presbyterians any truth?" he later asked. "Yes. Have the Baptists, Methodists, etc., any truth? Yes." He added that Latter-day Saints must "gather all the good and true prin-

ciples in the world and treasure them up" or they would not be "true 'Mormons.'" (*TPJS*, p. 316; *WJS*, p. 234.)

7. Backman, *First Vision*, p. 162.

8. See Porter, "Reverend George Lane," pp. 321–40. Another source reports that Joseph made his report to a Methodist. See Backman, *First Vision*, p. 177.

9. The 1838 account reports the man "saying it was all of the Devil, that there was no such thing as visions and revelations in these days" (Backman, *First Vision*, p. 164).

10. It has been pointed out that these stories radically contradict each other. On the one hand we read of a shiftless person who is always aimlessly telling stories and never doing a decent day's work, and on the other hand we read that every night at midnight he's out with a crew digging for silver or buried treasure and never finding it. That is hardly indolent. See Nibley, *The Myth Makers*, pp. 91–190.

11. See reported recollection of Mrs. Palmer in Cox, "Stories from Notebook of Martha Cox, Grandmother of Fern Cox," p. 1; also Madsen, "Guest Editor's Prologue," p. 235; Andrus, *They Knew The Prophet*, pp. 1–2.

12. The document says that "the boy was the best help he had ever found. . . . When Joseph Smith worked with them the work went steadily forward, and he got the full worth of the wages he paid." (As reported in Cox, "Stories from Notebook," p. 1; Madsen, "Prologue," p. 235; Andrus, *They Knew*, p. 1.)

13. Allen J. Stout recalls that as a member of the Nauvoo Legion he lamented to Joseph that he was quick to fight. The Prophet responded by speaking of his own youth and of learning to fight "much against his own will." His parents, Joseph said, had taught their family that quarreling and fighting are beastly sins. Whenever he "laid his hand in anger on a fellow creature it gave him sorrow and a feeling of shame." He added, however, that in the defense of righteousness or of the innocent he could "fight to the death." (Reported recollection of Allen J. Stout in Lee, Notebook, pp. 7–8.)

14. Mrs. Palmer recalls that the man who asked her father to break his ties with Joseph after he claimed a vision was "one of [our] church leaders," presumably a minister. She was a Presbyterian; presumably so was the leader. In any case, after the second vision she too turned against Joseph and her family "cut off their friendship for all the Smiths, for all

the family followed Joseph. Even the father, intelligent man that he was, could not discern the evil he was helping to promote." (As reported in Cox, "Stories from Notebook," p. 1; see Madsen, "Prologue," p. 235; Andrus, *They Knew*, pp. 1-2.)

15. "I was afraid my father would not believe me," Mother Smith recalls Joseph saying of Moroni's visits (*History of Joseph Smith by His Mother*, p. 79). Instead, as Joseph recalled in 1840 at his father's death, "He was the first person who received my testimony after I had seen the angel, and exhorted me to be faithful and diligent to the message I had received" (HC 4:190). Joseph was the fourth child, and yet the older brothers and his sisters Catherine and Sophronia sustained him. Samuel, who contracted a fever after being pursued by a mob on the night of the martyrdom, lost his life just thirty-three days after Joseph and Hyrum. Even many of Joseph's uncles and cousins, though not all of them, became dedicated members of the Church.

16. Joseph wrote of his father's response to Moroni's visitations: "He replied to me that it was of God, and told me to go and do as commanded by the messenger" (Joseph Smith—History 1:50).

17. "It seems as though the adversary was aware, at a very early period of my life, that I was destined to prove a disturber and an annoyer of his kingdom; else why should the powers of darkness combine against me? Why the opposition and persecution that arose against me, almost in my infancy?" (Joseph Smith—History 1:20.)

18. TPJS, p. 365; WJS, p. 367.

19. At this point he was, he wrote, "ready to sink into despair . . . not to an imaginary ruin, but to the power of some actual being from the unseen world" (Joseph Smith—History 1:16).

20. In the 1835 account he says, "My tongue seemed to be swollen in my mouth" (Backman, *First Vision*, p. 159). See also Joseph Smith—History 1:15.

21. See Moses 1:12-16.

22. TPJS, p. 181; WJS, p. 60.

23. TPJS, p. 187; WJS, p. 72.

24. Joseph taught that it is a mistake to underestimate the power of the evil one, as also to overestimate it. "Unless we in our hearts consent and yield—our organization [is] such that we can resist the devil. If we were not organized so, we would not be free agents." (WJS, p. 65.) Yet so powerful and pervasive has been the adversary's influence that, as the

Prophet taught John Bernhisel, "in every previous dispensation, Lucifer had prevailed and driven the priesthood from the earth. But in this last dispensation the reign of the Son of God and His priesthood was firmly established, nevermore to depart; thus all the inhabitants of the world might partake of the gifts and blessings of God." (Andrus, *They Knew*, p. 177.)

25. See, for example, his change from the word *fire* to *light* in the 1832 account (Backman, *First Vision*, p. 157).

26. P. 5.

27. See Backman, *First Vision*, p. 159.

28. See Backman, *First Vision*, p. 169.

29. John 14:8–9.

30. Alma 5:14, 19.

31. In Conference Report, October 1926, p. 112; *Gospel Ideals*, p. 355.

32. Recollection of Heber C. Kimball in Whitney, *Life of Heber C. Kimball*, p. 94; italics added.

33. *TPJS*, p. 368; *WJS*, p. 369.

34. "Verily, verily, I say unto you, The Son can do nothing of himself, but what he seeth the Father do: for what things soever he doeth, these also doeth the Son likewise" (John 5:19).

35. *Doctrines of Salvation* 1:32–33.

36. The Prophet stated in this discourse: "What did Jesus do? 'Why, I do the things that I saw the Father do when worlds came into existence. I saw the Father work out a kingdom with fear and trembling, and I can do the same.' " (*WJS*, p. 358.) In his final discourse in the Nauvoo grove he said: "The Savior says, 'The work that my Father did do I also.' And those are the works. He took himself a body and then laid down his life that he might take it up again." (*WJS*, p. 382.) Joseph spoke of these as "first principles of the gospel" (*WJS*, p. 358).

37. Joseph Smith—History 1:20. Compare his comment on the visit of Moroni: "He quoted many other passages of scripture, and offered many explanations which cannot be mentioned here" (Joseph Smith—History 1:41). Oliver Cowdery records that "our brother was permitted to see and understand much more full and perfect than I am able to communicate in writing" (MA 1 [April 1835]: 112).

38. Backman, *First Vision*, p. 159.

39. D&C 130:5.

40. "When I came to myself again, I found myself lying on my back, looking up into heaven" (Joseph Smith—History 1:20).

41. "For no man has seen God at any time in the flesh, except quickened by the Spirit of God" (D&C 67:11). "Flesh and blood cannot go there; but flesh and bones, quickened by the Spirit of God, can" (*TPJS*, p. 326).

42. "Joseph appeared as strong as a lion, but Sidney seemed as weak as water, and Joseph, noticing his condition smiled and said, 'Brother Sidney is not as used to it as I am' " (recollection of Philo Dibble in *Early Scenes in Church History*, p. 81).

43. "Comforted, I endeavored to arise but felt uncommon feeble." So Joseph told convert Alexander Neibaur, who conversed with the Prophet about the First Vision on May 24, 1844. (See Backman, *First Vision*, p. 177.)

44. *TPJS*, p. 345. In Joseph Smith's translation of the New Testament the Master's pronouncement, "I never knew you," is changed to, "Ye never knew me" (compare Matthew 7:23 and JST Matthew 7:33). See also JST Matthew 25:11, wherein the Lord tells the five foolish virgins, "Ye know me not."

45. *TPJS*, p. 149; *WJS*, p. 4.

46. See *WJS*, pp. 13-15.

47. "And he spake a parable unto them to this end, that men ought always to pray, and not to faint" (see Luke 18:1-8). The admonition to "pray always" occurs eight times in the Doctrine and Covenants.

48. *WJS*, p. 15.

49. The phrase, "nor trouble me any more concerning this matter," follows a rebuke to Martin Harris (D&C 5:29). "Let this suffice" are the Lord's words following a partial answer to Joseph's concern to know the time of the Second Coming (see D&C 130:14-17). "Trouble me no more," the Lord says after detailing the purposes of the Sabbath (D&C 59:22).

50. See Luke 24:11. The Joseph Smith Translation suggests that all the disciples had spoken ill of Jesus when under pressure and that all had doubts and fears. "They had spoken evil against him before the people; for they were afraid to confess him before men." After the Master's remarks about sin and forgiveness, they said among themselves, "We shall not be forgiven." But Jesus replied: "Whosoever shall speak a word

against the Son of man, and repenteth, it shall be forgiven him; but unto him who blasphemeth against the Holy Ghost, it shall not be forgiven him." (See JST Luke 12:10–12.)

51. Luke 24:41. The word for *joy* in Greek carries connotations of delight and gladness.

52. John 20:29.

53. It is taught frequently that the influence of the Holy Ghost is the ultimate source of assurance and certitude. The forces of evil simulate light; but their light is, comparatively speaking, darkness. See, for example, Brigham Young's remarks that "the spirit of truth will detect everything, and enable all who possess it to understand truth from error, light from darkness, the things of God from the things not of God" (*JD* 13:336).

54. From the 1832 account as found in Backman, *First Vision*, p. 157.

55. "For no man has seen God at any time in the flesh, except quickened by the Spirit of God. Neither can any natural man abide the presence of God, neither after the carnal mind. Ye are not able to abide the presence of God now, neither the ministering of angels; wherefore, continue in patience until ye are perfected." (D&C 67:11–13.)

56. "They seek not the Lord to establish his righteousness, but every man walketh in his own way, and after the image of his own god, whose image is in the likeness of the world, and whose substance is that of an idol. . . ." (D&C 1:16.)

57. A "principle of harmony"—an impersonal abstracton—can always be vaguely defined as forestalling any specific counsels, commandments, or corrections. It is a middle ground between a universal negation ("There is no God") and a personal affirmation ("There is a living and commanding God"). Advocacy, even worship, of such a principle is religion without costs.

58. *TPJS*, p. 286; *WJS*, p. 179. This statement was made on the thirteenth anniversary of the organization of the Church. The Prophet may have been contemplating how much turbulence had been crowded into those thirteen years.

59. D&C 5:22.

## Chapter 2. Joseph's Personality and Character

1. See, for example, the acknowledgment to "S. B. Sperry" under "Addenda et Corrigenda" in Brown, ed., *A Hebrew and English Lexicon of the Old Testament*, p. xii.

2. Wilford Woodruff remarked, "The people could not bear the flood of intelligence which God poured into his mind" (*JD* 5:83). Likewise George Q. Cannon stated: "I have sometimes thought that the Prophet Joseph, with the knowledge he possessed and the progress he had made could not stay with the people, so slow were we to comprehend things and so enshrouded in our ignorant traditions. The Saints could not comprehend Joseph Smith; the Elders could not; the Apostles could not. They did do a little towards the close of his life; but his knowledge was so extensive and his comprehension so great that they could not rise to it." (*MS* 61 [October 5, 1899]: 629.)

3. The Prophet's uncle John Smith stated, "The Prophet Joseph stood even six feet high in his stocking feet and weighed 212 pounds . . . Hyrum Smith stood five feet eleven and a half inches high and they weighed in the same notch, varying from 210 to 212 pounds" (*Salt Lake Herald*, January 12, 1895).

4. See Wirthlin, "Joseph Smith's Boyhood Operation: An 1813 Surgical Success," pp. 131–54.

5. Mary Elizabeth Rollins Lightner said in a late recollection that Joseph said to her, "I have asked the Lord to take me out of the world. I have stood all I can." (Sketch by Elsie E. Barrett, p. 16.)

6. John Taylor later took these casts to England, where a Mr. Gahagan, who created busts of the Duke of Wellington, Lord Nelson, and the Emperor of Russia, used them to make authentic busts of Joseph and Hyrum (see Cannon, *George Cannon the Immigrant*, p. 131; also letter of John Taylor in *MS* 12 [November 1, 1850]: 329–30).

7. Jane Snyder Richards, for example, who met him first when he was thirty-seven in Nauvoo, wrote that "his hair was of a light brown, blue eyes and light-complexioned" ("Reminiscences of Mrs. F. D. Richards," p. 11). Compare the statement of Wandle Mace who wrote that Joseph had a "light complexion, blue eyes, and light hair, and very little beard" (journal of Wandle Mace, p. 37). James Palmer noted: "He wore no whiskers" (journal of James Palmer, p. 70).

8. Elam Chenery uses the phrase "no breakage about his body" (see *YWJ* 17 [December 1906]: 539-40). Compare James Palmer's description:

"He had a large full chest and intelligent eyes and fine limbs" (journal of James Palmer, p. 282). A non-Mormon visitor in 1843 said, "Joe Smith the Mormon Prophet is a large tolerably good looking man 38 years of age—light hair light eyes nothing very extraordinary in his appearance . . . possessed of the most astonishing degree of vanity" (see diary of J. M. Sharpe [1843–48]).

9. He defeated the strongest wrestler of Davies County, throwing him three times (see *Autobiography of Andrew Jenson*, p. 161; also pp. 164–65). Edwin Holden said he could play until the boys tired of the games and then unite all together to build a log cabin (*JI* 27 [March 1, 1892]: 153). He wrestled for exercise. When he sent Jacob Gates on a mission he said, "Go and fill your mission, and we will wrestle after you come back" (Jenson, *Latter-day Saint Biographical Encyclopedia* 1:198).

10. "Often after a heated discussion with ministers over doctrinal points, the prophet would say, 'Gentlemen, let's lay the scriptures aside for a moment and I'll challenge you to jump at the mark with me' " (Barrett, *Joseph Smith, the Extraordinary*, p. 9). In Nauvoo, Saturday afternoons were the time for races, jumping at a mark, pulling up stakes, wrestling, and throwing (see Anderson, ed., *Joseph Smith III and the Restoration*, p. 27).

11. "In the evening, when pulling sticks, I pulled up Justus A. Morse, the strongest man in Ramus, with one hand" (*HC* 5:302; see also p. 466).

12. See recollection of Calvin W. Moore in *JI* 27 (April 15, 1892): 255.

13. *History of Joseph Smith*, p. 82.

14. See Zucker, "Joseph Smith as a Student of Hebrew," pp. 41–55.

15. Seixas came to Kirtland from Hudson, Ohio, and began his school on January 26, 1836, continuing for two months. By that time "only two of the class knew enough Hebrew to discuss it or to discourse on Hebrew phraseology from the Bible, Joseph Smith and Orson Pratt" (Berrett, *Joseph Smith, Symbol of Greatness*, p. 3). Hebrew and Latin were taught over a period of six months. Lorenzo Barnes writes: "I obtained considerable information of the Hebrew and Chaldaic languages so I could read and translate tolerably well" (see journal of Lorenzo Barnes, vol. 2). The Prophet also worked sporadically in Greek, Latin, and German.

16. Though Heber C. Kimball saw himself as "illiterate and unlearned, weak and feeble," he became one of the most powerful and fruit-

ful missionaries in modern history. See the letter to his son William in foreword to Young, *Letters of Brigham Young to His Sons*, p. xii.

17. *TPJS*, p. 137; *HC* 3:295.

18. See D&C 121, 122, and 123. The entire letter is published in *HC* 3:289–305 and in *TPJS*, pp. 129–48.

19. *TPJS*, p. 137.

20. *TPJS*, p. 137.

21. He records there were "little variation[s]," i.e., differences, in citations from Malachi; but that the verses in Acts 3:22 and 23 were quoted "precisely as they stand in our New Testament." Either he had memorized these verses and could recognize "little variations" as he heard them or he remembered exactly how they were spoken and later read or reread them in the Bible and noticed the variations. Either way, he had a precise memory. See Joseph Smith—History 1:36–41.

22. One acquaintance of Joseph claims he could "read over a passage of scripture three times and one year after reading it he could quote it verbatim and open the book to the portion quoted" (Elijah Knapp Fuller, according to a grandson, told to N.B. Lundwall, "Lundwall Microfilm Collection," Reel 2-55).

23. D&C 132:7.

24. See William Clayton's testimony of February 16, 1874 as cited in Jenson, *The Historical Record* 6:224–26. Joseph F. Smith, among others, asserts that from 1831 Joseph understood plural marriage would be introduced in modern times. On July 12, 1843, he was encouraged by Hyrum to put it on paper. "Joseph said he knew it from beginning to end. He then dictated it word for word to Wm. Clayton as it is now in the Doctrine and Covenants. . . . After it was done Joseph said, 'There, that is enough for the present, but I have a great deal more.' " (Utah Stake Historical Record, March 3 and 4, 1883. See also comments of Orson Pratt in *JD* 13:183–96; *CHC* 2:100–101.)

25. Minerva Wade Hickman wrote, "The mind of the Prophet Joseph Smith was as clear as crystal. He cleared up the difficulties of ages" ("Sketch of Minerva Wade Hickman," May 30, 1842). Emmeline B. Wells wrote in retrospect: "He was beyond my comprehension" (*YWJ* 16 [December 1905]: 556). Mercy R. Thompson wrote, "I have seen him in the lyceum [in Nauvoo] and heard him reprove the brethren for giving way to too much excitement and warmth in debate, and have listened to his clear and masterly explanations of deep and difficult questions. To him

all things seemed simple and easy to be understood, and thus he could make them plain to others as no other man could that I ever heard." (*JI* 27 [July 1, 1892]: 399.) Jedediah M. Grant said: "Why was it that Joseph could take the wisest Elder that ever travelled and preached, and, as it were, circumscribe his very thoughts? Simply because he had the Holy Ghost." (*JD* 3:10.)

26. Contrasting Joseph Smith's literary style with Oliver Cowdery's "flowery journalese," Arthur Henry King continues: "I am asked sometimes, 'Why don't we have any great literature now?' And we don't, you know; we may kid ourselves or other people may try to kid us that we do, but we don't. There were Homer, Vergil, Dante, Shakespeare, and Goethe; and there it seems to have stopped. There seems to have been no supreme figure since then. But I tell you there was one: Joseph Smith." (See "Joseph Smith As a Writer," in *The Abundance of the Heart*, pp. 197–205.)

27. The *Timaeus*, one of Plato's last dialogues, deals with cosmology, the relationship of *nous*, or mind, to the soul and the soul to the body. It also presupposes complex theories of the nature of truth, and of universals (ultimate ideas) in abstraction. Section 93 was received in May, 1833, when Joseph was twenty-seven years old. It defines beginningless beginnings, the interrelationships of truth, of light, of intelligence, of agency, of element, of embodiment, of joy. Every sentence, every word, is freighted with meaning. In one fell swoop it cuts many Gordian knots. For example: How can there something come from nothing? Answer: The universe was not created from nothing. "The elements are eternal." How can Christ have been both absolutely human and absolutely divine at the same time? Answer: He was not both at the same time. Christ "received not of the fulness at the first, but continued . . . until he received a fulness." If man is totally the creation of God, how can he be anything or do anything that he was not divinely pre-caused to do? Answer: Man is not totally the creation of God. "Intelligence . . . was not created or made, neither indeed can be. . . . Behold, here is the agency of man." How can man be a divine creation and yet be "totally depraved"? Answer: Man is not totally depraved. "Every spirit of man was innocent in the beginning; and God having redeemed man from the fall, men became again, in their infant state, innocent before God." What is the relationship of being and beings, the one and the many? Answer: "Being" is only the collective name of beings, of whom God is one. Truth is knowledge of things (plural), and not, as Plato would have it, of Thinghood.

"Truth is knowledge of things as they are, and as they were, and as they are to come." How can spirit relate to gross matter? Answer: "The elements are the tabernacle of God." Why should man be embodied? Answer: "Spirit and element, inseparably connected, receive a fulness of joy." If we begin susceptible to light and truth, how is it that people err and abuse the light? Answer: People are free; they can be persuaded only if they choose to be. They cannot be compelled. The Socratic thesis that knowledge is virtue (that if you really know the good you will seek it and do it) is mistaken. It is through disobedience and because of the traditions of the fathers that light is taken away from mankind.

28. Joseph Smith—History 1:28.

29. Rachel R. Grant, with many others, remarks that "he was always so jolly and happy. . . . He was different in that respect from Brother Hyrum, who was more sedate, more serious." (*YWJ* 16 [December 1905]: 551.) Because of this spontaneity he sometimes had to warn the people that his manner should not be taken as flippant or irresponsible: "The Saints need not think because I am familiar with them and am playful and cheerful, that I am ignorant of what is going on. Iniquity of any kind cannot be sustained in the Church, and it will not fare well where I am; for I am determined while I do lead the Church, to lead it right." (May 27, 1843, HC 5:411.)

30. See discourse of George A. Smith in *JD* 2:214.

31. "Which one of you can beat that?" So Wilford Woodruff remembers him saying. (See Parry, comp., *Stories About Joseph Smith the Prophet*, pp. 17–18.)

32. Recalled by Jedediah M. Grant in *JD* 3:67.

33. See recollection of Daniel D. McArthur in *JI* 27 (February 15, 1892): 129; Andrus, *They Knew*, pp. 73–74. George A. Smith, speaking of another similar incident, says that Joseph told the man "he ought not to give way to such an enthusiastic spirit, and bray so much like a jackass" (*JD* 2:214).

34. The context of this statement is that "what many people call sin is not sin" (*TPJS*, p. 193; *WJS*, p. 80). At other times Joseph had to teach that what many people called righteous was not righteous and what many assumed was acceptable to God was not acceptable. He once stunned a congregation in Nauvoo by describing a man's two-hour sermon as "pharisaical and hypocritical and not edifying the people." The

man (William Clark) accepted the reproof and stayed with the Church. (7 November 1841, *WJS*, p. 80.)

35. From an 1842 address to the Relief Society, *WJS*, p. 130. This occurred at the time of John C. Bennett's defection and much slanderous publicity.

36. *JI* 27 (February 15, 1892): 129; Andrus, *They Knew*, p. 73.

37. See experiences of Edwin Rushton as related by his son in Andrus, *They Knew*, p. 170. Edwin Rushton was seventeen when he reached Nauvoo on April 13, 1842.

38. "I told them I was but a man, and they must not expect me to be perfect; if they expected perfection from me, I should expect it from them" (*TPJS*, p. 268; *WJS*, p. 132). Elsewhere he said that though he was "subject to like passions as other men, like the prophets of olden times," he was "under the necessity of bearing the infirmities of others" (*HC* 5:516).

39. *HC* 5:265; *TPJS*, p. 278.

40. *HC* 5:390-91.

41. See Evans, *Joseph Smith: An American Prophet*, p. 9.

42. *TPJS*, p. 225; *WJS*, p. 116.

43. "Sketch of My Life," *The Relief Society Magazine* 31 (March 1944): 134.

44. It is possible, if not likely, that the following lines penned by Eliza R. Snow were addressed to Joseph Smith:

> And when I saw your towering soul
> Rise on devotion's wings:
> And saw amid your pulses, roll,
> A scorn of trifling things,
> I loved you for your goodness' sake
> And cheerfully can part
> With home and friends, confiding in
> Your noble, generous heart.

(From "Narcissa to Narcissus" in Snow, *Poems: Religious, Historical, and Political* 2:47–48.)

45. Eliza wrote of him: "Though his expansive mind grasped the great plan of salvation and solved the mystic problem of man's destiny—though he had in his possession keys that unlocked the past

and the future with its succession of eternities, in his devotions he was humble as a little child" ("Sketch of My Life," p. 136).

46. See recollection of Mary Ann Winters in *YWJ* 16 (December 1905): 557; Andrus, *They Knew*, p. 166. Mary remembered that Joseph said, "Brother Parley, you have come home, bringing your sheaves with you," and that tears rolled down his cheeks. Willard Richards wrote that on this occasion Joseph "appeared melted in tenderness when he met Sister Pratt (who had been to England with Parley) and her little daughter only three or four days old" (see entry of April 12, 1843, in Joseph Smith journal, March 10, 1843 to July 14, 1843, kept by Willard Richards; *HC* 5:354).

47. D&C 21:7–8.

48. *TPJS*, p. 304; *WJS*, p. 205.

49. See recollection of O. B. Huntington in *YWJ* 4 (April 1893): 321.

50. *WJS*, p. 196.

51. *TPJS*, p. 361; *WJS*, p. 343.

52. *TPJS*, p. 306.

53. *TPJS*, p. 195.

54. See D&C 25.

55. Mother Smith wrote of Emma: "I have never seen a woman in my life, who would endure every species of fatigue and hardship, from month to month, and from year to year, with that unflinching courage, zeal, and patience, which she has ever done; for I know that which she has had to endure—she has been tossed upon the ocean of uncertainty —she has breasted the storms of persecution, and buffeted the rage of men and devils, which would have borne down almost any other woman" (*History of Joseph Smith*, p. 191).

56. "Three times a day he had family worship; and these precious seasons of sacred household service truly seemed a foretaste of celestial happiness" (recollection of Eliza R. Snow in Tullidge, *The Women of Mormondom*, p. 66). In this custom Joseph followed his own admonition: "You must make yourselves acquainted with those men who like Daniel pray three times a day toward the House of the Lord" (*HC* 3:391). William H. Walker described coming to the front door of the Mansion House one evening and overhearing the singing of the Prophet's family: "I had never heard such sweet, heavenly music, and I was equally impressed with the prayer offered by the Prophet" (see sketch of William H. Walker in

Walker and Stevenson, comps., *Ancestry and Descendants of John Walker*, p. 15).

57. See recollection of Jesse W. Crosby as reported in Cox, "Stories from Notebook," pp. 1–2. See also Andrus, *They Knew*, p. 145.

58. Lorin Farr says of the Prophet: "There was another thing about him: When he went to bed he slept. He was not nervous. He figured broadly, but when he had done a day's work he dismissed it from his mind. It was thus that the next day he was ready for other things." (Quoted in Pardoe, *Lorin Farr, Pioneer*, p. 292.)

59. D&C 21:1.

60. Joseph weighed over 200 pounds. Coray, twelve years younger, weighed 130 pounds. In the wake of Coray's request Joseph asked his father, Joseph, Sr., to give Coray a patriarchal blessing. He himself, looking at Coray earnestly, promised "You will soon find a companion, one that will be suited to your condition. . . . She will cling to you like the cords of death; and you will have a good many children." Coray later married Martha Knowlton. They had seven sons and five daughters. (See Coray, Autobiographical sketches, pp. 8–9; Andrus, *They Knew*, pp. 135–36.)

61. Robert B. Thompson, says Huntington, was "never guilty of such an impropriety" as to go on a "good spree." He was dead within two weeks of the Prophet's prediction. (See diary of Oliver B. Huntington, p. 166.)

62. "He did not want it strung up all the time" (see recollection of William M. Allred in *JI* 27 [August 1, 1892]: 472). On the other hand, Joseph observed: "When a man is reigned up continually by excitement, he becomes strong and gains power and knowledge; but when he relaxes for a season he loses much of his power and knowledge" (*HC* 5:389).

63. This took place in 1841, at the home of the Henry Sherwoods in Nauvoo. (See recollection of Henrietta Cox in *JI* 27 [April 1, 1892]: 203; Andrus, *They Knew*, p. 147.)

64. *WJS*, p. 162.

65. Recollection of John Lyman Smith in *JI* (March 15, 1892): 172.

66. Peter H. Burnett acted as a defending attorney for the Mormons during the Missouri period. He later wrote of Joseph: "He was much more than an ordinary man. He possessed the most indomitable perseverance, was a good judge of men, and deemed himself born to command, and he

did command. His views were so strange and striking, and his manner was so earnest, and apparently so candid, that you could not but be interested. There was a kind, familiar look about him, that pleased you. He was very courteous in discussion, readily admitting what he did not intend to controvert, and would not oppose you abruptly, but had due deference to your feelings. He had the capacity for discussing a subject in different aspects, and for proposing many original views, even of ordinary matters. His illustrations were his own. He had great influence over others. As an evidence of this I will state that on Thursday, just before I left to return to Liberty [Missouri], I saw him out among the crowd, conversing freely with every one, and seeming to be perfectly at ease. In the short space of five days he had managed so to mollify his enemies that he could go unprotected among them without the slightest danger. Among the Mormons he had much greater influence than Sidney Rigdon. The latter was a man of superior education, an eloquent speaker, of fine appearance and dignified manners; but he did not possess the native intellect of Smith, and lacked his determined will." (*An Old California Pioneer*, p. 40.) Compare the comments of another attorney, Joseph Kelting: "Joseph was a mighty man and borrowed from no one; he was original and inspiring in his talk" (see Joseph Smith Papers).

67. According to the relation of an incident by Anson Call recorded by Abraham H. Cannon, Stephen A. Douglas once remarked: "Joseph Smith is the only independent man I ever saw. We are always wondering what effect our actions will have upon our constituents or friends, but he does what he thinks is right regardless of what people think or say of him." (See entry of March 9, 1890, in diary of Abraham H. Cannon, December 29, 1889 to July 15, 1890, pp. 89–90; compare journal of Wandle Mace, p. 285.)

68. See incidents in HC 3:190 and following pages.

69. The exact quotation reads: "I do not think that Joe Smith was at heart a bad or wicked man, and you could see from his face that he was not naturally an unkind one" (*Iowa Democrat*, May 13, 1885).

70. As recalled by Jesse N. Smith in *Journal of Jesse Nathaniel Smith*, p. 456. Wells had a superior legal education for this period.

71. Comparing Joseph and Hyrum, Brigham Young remarked: "His [Hyrum's] integrity was of the highest order, but his ability was not equal to Joseph's. Hyrum was a positive man; Joseph was a comparative man, regarding everything according to the circumstances of the case and every

person according to the intrinsic worth." (See unpublished discourse of October 8, 1866, Church Archives, The Church of Jesus Christ of Latter-day Saints, Salt Lake City, Utah.)

72. "To become a joint heir of the heirship of the Son," Joseph said in 1843, "one must put away all his false traditions" (*TPJS*, p. 321; *WJS*, p. 244).

## Chapter 3. Joseph Smith and Spiritual Gifts

1. *TPJS*, p. 270.

2. *Masterful Discourses and Writings of Orson Pratt*, p. 570.

3. *TPJS*, p. 328; *WJS*, p. 256.

4. D&C 46:8–9.

5. D&C 46:9.

6. D&C 46:29.

7. *TPJS*, p. 162; *WJS*, p. 12.

8. D&C 46:13.

9. James 1:6–7.

10. D&C 46:14; italics added.

11. "Every word that proceedeth from the mouth of Jehovah has such an influence over the human mind—the logical mind—that it is convincing without other testimony. Faith cometh by hearing." (*WJS*, p. 237.)

12. "I have felt since, that I felt much like Paul" (Joseph Smith—History 1:24). "I, like Paul, have been in perils" (*WJS*, p. 373). Pauline phraseology is sprinkled throughout his sermons and writings. Yet he said, "Peter penned the most sublime language of any of the apostles" (*TPJS*, p. 301; *WJS*, p. 202).

13. Eleven hundred statements about the future appear in the Doctrine and Covenants alone. Seven hundred are "of a spiritual nature" and many are conditional; for example, "It shall come to pass that he that asketh in Spirit shall receive in Spirit." The remaining four hundred deal "more directly with things of earth." (See Widtsoe, *Joseph Smith: Seeker After Truth, Prophet of God*, p. 277.)

14. An annotated list of three thousand Mormon journals, mostly of the first and second generations, has been compiled by Davis Bitton in his *Guide to Mormon Diaries and Autobiographies*. It is a compendium of prophetic incidents.

15. Recollections of Daniel Tyler in *JI* 27 (February 15, 1892): 127.

16. See recollection of Daniel Tyler in *JI* 27 (February 15, 1892): 127–28.

17. Heber C. Kimball writes: "I have heard Joseph say many times that he was much tempted about the revelations the Lord gave through him—it seemed to be so impossible for them to be fulfilled" (cited in Whitney, *Life of Heber C. Kimball*, pp. 391–92).

18. See recollection of Daniel Tyler in *JI* 27 (February 15, 1892): 128. Once as Joseph spoke in the grove west of the unfinished temple he was interrupted by rain and hail. The people began to run for cover. Joseph called to them to sit down and pray that the Lord would stay the winds and the storm. They did so, and the Prophet spoke for an hour and a half, untouched by the downpour that continued nearby but not in the grove. (See journal of Amasa Potter, p. 494.) A similar account is given by Mary C. Westover in *YWJ* 17 (December 1906): 545. This may have been the occasion of the King Follett discourse.

19. See *TPJS*, p. 269; compare p. 289.

20. See *TPJS*, p. 121; *HC* 3:30.

21. *TPJS*, p. 308.

22. See recollection of William G. Nelson in *YWJ* 17 (December 1906): 543. Ezra T. Clark recalled: "I heard the Prophet Joseph say he would give the Saints a key whereby they would never be led away or deceived, and that was: the Lord would never suffer the majority of this people to be led away or deceived by imposters, nor would he allow the records of this Church to fall into the hands of the enemy" (*IE* 5 [January 1902]: 202). Edward Stevenson remembered the statement as "a key by which you may never be deceived" and that it was that "a majority of the saints and the records and history of the Church also" would remain with the Church (see Jenson and Stevenson, *Infancy of the Church*, p. 5).

23. The least spectacular but most personal prophecy of Joseph is this: "If you will obey the Gospel with honest hearts, I promise you in the name of the Lord, that the gifts as promised by our Saviour will follow you, and by this you may prove me to be a true servant of God" (as re-

called by Edward Stevenson in his *Reminiscences of Joseph, the Prophet, and the Coming Forth of the Book of Mormon*, p. 4).

24. *YWJ* 2 (November 1890): 81. One can refuse to bear (beget) children. And one can refuse to bear (love and nurture) begotten children. Both refusals are epidemic in our time.

25. See *TPJS*, p. 255.

26. "You will build cities to the North and to the South, and to the East and to the West; and you will become a great and wealthy people in that land" ("Life Story of Mosiah Lyman Hancock," pp. 27–29; compare the phrase, "a large and wealthy people," in Mosiah 27:7). The statement that the people would be tried by riches more than by poverty is remembered by Angus M. Cannon in *The Deseret Weekly*, January 11, 1890, p. 103.

27. *JD* 10:297; *Discourses of Brigham Young*, p. 471.

28. See Snow, "Sketch of My Life," *The Relief Society Magazine* 31 (September 1944): 504.

29. *HC* 5:601.

30. See journal of John Lyman Smith, p. 7.

31. See diary of Oliver B. Huntington, vol. 2, p. 168; Andrus, *They Knew*, pp. 65–66.

32. "Brother Joseph," said William, "you were right to come. You get in my bed and don't you worry. The Lord will protect you." In the light of dawn the mob saw their mistake. "When Brother Joseph saw what they had done [to William] he clasped him in his arms and said, 'Brother William, in the name of the Lord I promise you will never taste of death.'" (See diary of Oliver B. Huntington, p. 9.)

33. William Huntington went west with the exodus and settled eventually in Springville, Utah. One night, forty-three years after the Nauvoo incident, just after going to bed he was conversing with his wife in the darkness. He said something and she replied. She said something and he did not reply. After two or three repetitions she lighted a lamp. Without a sigh or a shudder he had died. The family believed this was the fulfillment of Joseph's promise, which is universalized in the Doctrine and Covenants: "And it shall come to pass that those that die in me shall not taste of death, for it shall be sweet unto them; and they that die not in me, wo unto them, for their death is bitter" (D&C 42:46–47). See diary of Oliver B. Huntington, vol. 2, p. 271, entry of March 19, 1887.

34. *The Discourses of Wilford Woodruff*, pp. 38–39. This happened in Kirtland in 1834. Wilford Woodruff recalled that each of the brethren bore five-minute testimonies and were then told by the Prophet that "they did not have any idea of the magnitude of the work in which they are engaged. It will go to the Rocky Mountains, and will eventually fill all of North and South America. When this prediction was made we were all in a little log cabin." It was fourteen feet square and held "all the priesthood in that city." Another journal says it took place in Father Johnson's home, one room, twelve-by-fourteen feet. (See Wilford Woodruff, cited in journal of Abraham H. Cannon, entry of April 19, 1894, p. 86. See also diary of Oliver B. Huntington, vol. 2, p. 211.)

35. JD 2:360.

36. TPJS, p. 162.

37. TPJS, p. 301.

38. JI 27 (January 1, 1892): 24. See also *Journal of Jesse Nathaniel Smith*, pp. 454–56.

39. See Cowley, *Wilford Woodruff: History of His Life and Labors*, p. 68. This took place during the financial distress in Kirtland in 1837.

40. See diary of Oliver B. Huntington, vol. 2, pp. 169–70. Joseph related this incident to Huntington two days after it occurred. The man was an adventurer named Joseph H. Jackson. His name appears on almost every page of the account of the Carthage tragedy. See, for example, Thomas Gregg's account in HC 6:149 and John Taylor's in Appendix 4 of Roberts, *The Rise and Fall of Nauvoo*, p. 455.

41. HC 1:317. The letter was to W. W. Phelps, who, as he later acknowledged, was not being completely forthright in his letters.

42. John Taylor says Joseph taught: "A man may have the gift of the discernment of spirits; he may see what is in the heart; but because that has been revealed to him he has no business to bring that as a charge against any person. The man's acts must be proved by evidence and by witnesses." (JD 26:359; *The Gospel Kingdom*, p. 202.)

43. See O. B. Huntington, in YWJ 5 (July 1894): 490–91.

44. See unpublished discourse of Brigham Young, October 8, 1866, Church Archives, The Church of Jesus Christ of Latter-day Saints, Salt Lake City, Utah.

45. As cited in Cowley, *Wilford Woodruff*, p. 226.

46. Journal of Levi Ward Hancock, p. 75; Andrus, *They Knew*, p. 19.

47. See *TPJS*, p. 369.

48. John Taylor says of Law that, though a counselor to Joseph in the First Presidency, he became "his most bitter foe and maligner"; that it was afterwards shown he had conspired with some Missourians to take Joseph Smith's life, and that he made the attempt. See affidavit in Journal History for 10 June 1844; Roberts, *Rise and Fall*, p. 406. The Laws threatened to destroy the Temple (see journal of William Clayton, 1841–44, p. 47).

49. *WJS*, p. 196.

50. *JD* 10:148. On the Prophet's feelings of frustration in teaching, see John Taylor in *JD* 1:176 and 21:94; Wilford Woodruff in *JD* 5:83; and George Q. Cannon in *MS* 61 (October 5, 1899): 629.

51. "We frequently see some of them, after suffering all they have for the work of God, will fly to pieces like glass as soon as anything comes that is contrary to their traditions; they cannot stand the fire at all" (*TPJS*, p. 331; *WJS*, p. 319).

52. *TPJS*, p. 331; *WJS*, p. 319.

53. *HC* 5:139.

54. *TPJS*, p. 305.

55. *TPJS*, p. 296; *WJS*, p. 196.

56. *TPJS*, p. 191; *WJS*, p. 77.

57. *TPJS*, p. 161; *WJS*, p. 12.

58. *TPJS*, p. 291; *WJS*, p. 185.

59. *HC* 5:247.

60. *WJS*, p. 59.

61. *D&C* 128:20–21. These verses name Moroni; Peter, James, and John; Michael; Gabriel; Raphael; and Michael, or Adam.

62. In addition to the Father and the Son, John Taylor names Abraham, Isaac, Jacob, Noah, Adam, Seth, Enoch, and the Apostles that lived on this continent as well as those who lived on the Asiatic continent (*JD* 21:94).

63. See Joseph Young, *Enoch and His City*, pp. 10–11; *HC* 1:297. Compare *HC* 1:323.

64. As recalled by M. Isabella Horne in "Joseph Smith a True Prophet," *YWJ* 31 (April 1920): 211–12.

65. *YWJ* 10 (January 1899): 22.

66. See "A Day of God's Power" in Roberts, *Rise and Fall*, pp. 39–42. Compare CHC 2:18–22; HC 4:3–5.

67. HC 4:3.

68. See records of Heber C. Kimball, Parley P. Pratt, and Brigham Young, Church Archives, The Church of Jesus Christ of Latter-day Saints, Salt Lake City, Utah.

69. "Let the elders either obtain the power of God to heal the sick, or let them cease to minister the forms without the power" (as quoted in *Autobiography of Parley P. Pratt*, p. 294).

70. "I used once to be troubled with dyspepsia and had frequently to call upon the Elders to administer, and on one occasion, brother Joseph Smith says to me, 'Brother Grant, if I could always be with you, I could cure you' " (Jedediah M. Grant, in *JD* 3:12).

71. This occurred in Greenville, Indiana, where Joseph was caring for Newell K. Whitney, whose leg had been broken in a carriage accident. Joseph replaced his own dislocated jaw with his hands, went to the bedside of Bishop Whitney to receive an administration, and was healed. (See Jenson, *Biographical Encyclopedia*: 1:225.)

72. George A. Smith wrote that Joseph said "a severe scourge would come upon the camp, and many would die like sheep with rot" (see Jarvis, *Ancestry, Biography and Family of George A. Smith*, pp. 48–51). Edson Barney recalled him as saying that "some of them would die off like rotten sheep" (*JI* 27 [April 15, 1892]: 256). Zera Cole and Jacob Gates likewise speak of it as a "scourge" (see Jacob Gates, *The Deseret News Weekly*, April 11, 1891).

73. When Joseph and Hyrum returned from Zion's Camp, they sat down with Mother Smith, each took one of her hands, and they recounted this healing which occurred when Hyrum had a vision of Mother Smith praying for them (see *History of Joseph Smith*, pp. 227–29).

74. See D&C 46:17–18.

75. *TPJS*, p. 287.

76. Journal of Edward Stevenson, p. 157; Andrus, *They Knew*, p. 87.

77. Cowley, *Wilford Woodruff*, p. 68.

78. *JD* 3:10.

79. D&C 100:10.

80. As recalled to the author by T. Earl Pardoe, author of the book *Lorin Farr, Pioneer*.

81. "Joseph Smith, the Prophet and Seer of the Lord, has done more, save Jesus only, for the salvation of men in this world, than any other man that ever lived in it" (D&C 135:3). This statement was written by John Taylor after the martyrdom.

82. *HC* 2:170.

83. *TPJS*, p. 161.

84. *TPJS*, p. 365.

85. The statement of the First Presidency says in part: "The great religious leaders of the world such as Mohammed, Confucius, and the Reformers, as well as philosophers including Socrates, Plato, and others, received a portion of God's light. Moral truths were given to them by God to enlighten whole nations and to bring a higher level of understanding to individuals." (Cited in Palmer, *The Expanding Church*, p. v.)

86. *TPJS*, p. 316; *WJS*, p. 234.

87. D&C 107:18–19.

88. See journal of Wilford Woodruff for instances.

89. This according to Addison Everett, who says Joseph had this conversation with the justice while waiting for trial at Colesville (see *YWJ* 2 [November 1890]: 75–76).

90. D&C 113:4.

91. This was Martha Knowlton Coray, whose husband records: "I have frequently heard her say that he [Joseph] himself was the greatest miracle to her she had ever seen; and that she valued her acquaintance with him above almost everything else" (Coray, Autobiographical sketches, p. 11).

## Chapter 4. Joseph Smith and Trials

1. D&C 24:8.

2. D&C 127:2. Edward Stevenson recalled, "I have often heard him say, 'I love to swim in deep water'" (see J. Grant Stevenson, "Life of Edward Stevenson . . . ," p. 104).

3. D&C 127:2.

4. See Smith, *History of Joseph Smith*, pp. 308–13.

5. D&C 5:22.

6. D&C 6:30.

7. The divine word to Joseph in Liberty Jail was, "And then, if thou endure it well, God shall exalt thee on high; thou shalt triumph over all thy foes" (D&C 121:8).

8. *TPJS*, p. 42.

9. Daniel Tyler heard this discourse in Far West, Missouri. See *JI* 27 (February 15, 1892): 128.

10. In 1834 Joseph himself said, "From apostates the faithful have received the severest persecutions" (*TPJS*, p. 67). As the Church grew, so did the severity of such opposition.

11. Recalled by Daniel Tyler in *JI* 27 (August 15, 1892): 492; Andrus, *They Knew*, p. 54. See also the Prophet's statement, "When once that light which was in them is taken from them, they become as much darkened as they were previously enlightened, and then, no marvel, if all their power should be enlisted against the truth" (*TPJS*, p. 67). Compare the statement of Jesus: "If . . . the light that is in thee [the disciples] be darkness, how great is that darkness!" (Matthew 6:23.) Joseph also said: "When you find a spirit that wants bloodshed—murder—the same is not of God, but is of the devil. Out of the abundance of the heart of man the mouth speaketh." (*TPJS*, p. 358.)

12. Smith, *History of Joseph Smith*, p. 320.

13. D&C 122:5.

14. See the author's pamphlet, *Joseph Smith Among the Prophets.*

15. See the first published accounts of this experience in *TS* 5 (August 15, 1844): 611–12, and in *MS* 14 (May 1, 1852): 148–50; see also Barrett, *Joseph Smith and the Restoration*, p. 205, and *MS* 26 (December 31, 1864): 834–35.

16. Benjamin F. Johnson reported that a dentist helped with Joseph's tooth problem "a year or two previous to his death." Until then "there had been a whistle-like sound" in his speaking. (See *The Benjamin F. Johnson Letter to George S. Gibbs*, p. 22.)

17. HC 5:442.

18. *TPJS*, p. 197; *WJS*, p. 106.

19. This statement is made by Brigham Young and apparently ascribed to "Elder Jos. Smith." (See record of the Utah Stake of Zion, July 17, 1868; also "Early History of Provo, 1849–72," vol. 2.)

20. In modern revelation we read that during the Millennium children will grow up without sin unto salvation (D&C 45:58). But at the end, Satan will be loosed again "for a little season" (see D&C 88:111). For a further discussion of this subject see the author's comment in Palmer, ed., *Deity and Death*, p. 65; also Smith, *Doctrines of Salvation* 2:54.

21. See recollection of Margarette McIntire Burgess in *JI* 27 (January 15, 1892): 67.

22. Mercy R. Thompson, wife of Joseph's scribe, Robert B. Thompson, recalled Joseph alighting from the carriage and picking flowers for her little girl (*JI* 27 [July 1, 1892]: 399). Joseph would pull the children up, "take them up in his arms and wash the mud from their bare feet with his handkerchief. And oh how kind he was to the old folks, as well as to little children." ("Life Story of Mosiah Lyman Hancock," p. 3.) In one of his last discourses Joseph said, "I rejoice in hearing the testimony of my aged friends" (*WJS*, p. 355).

23. See journal of Harvey H. Cluff, p. 6. Cluff recorded that this was "the first impression of divinity" of the Prophet's calling. He treated the young men as equals. An eleven-year-old, Alvah Alexander, was playing with Joseph's family when the Prophet came back with two men from the violence and abuse of his attempted kidnapping at Dixon (see *HC* 5:439–60). "These men had been arrested for abusing Joseph," Alvah later recalled. "He brought them in and treated them as he would one who had never done him a wrong; gave them their dinner before he would allow them to depart." During introductions, the Prophet pointed to Alvah, saying, "This is a neighbor's little boy." Alvah also recalled that "no amusements or games were as interesting to [him] as to hear [Joseph] talk." (*YWJ* 17 [December 1906]: 541.)

24. Journal of Amasa Potter, pp. 9–10.

25. "My family," he wrote, "was kept in a continual state of alarm, not knowing, when I went from home, that I should ever return again; or what would befall me from day to day" (*TS* 1 [November 1839]: 3).

26. One of these little girls was Sarah Holmes, daughter of Jonathan Holmes. She would sometimes "stand guard" sitting on a woodpile. When the "enemy" was a friend, Joseph would take Sarah in his arms, stand holding the door knob, and say, "Now, Sarah does that look like the mob?" then kiss her and put her down. (See Jonathan H. Holmes papers.)

27. Joseph himself records in July 1843: "This made the 38th vexatious lawsuit against me for my religion" (*HC* 5:518). After the kidnap-

ping incident at Dixon in 1843, Joseph told George Laub that this was the forty-second suit brought against him (see diary of George Laub, p. 18). Brigham Young said in one discourse that the lawsuits against Joseph totalled forty-six; in another, he said forty-seven (JD 14:199; JD 8:16).

28. Recollection of Patriarch Emer Harris, brother of Martin Harris, Church Archives, The Church of Jesus Christ of Latter-day Saints, Salt Lake City, Utah.

29. See Acts 17:6; 19:29–41; 21:31, 38.

30. "Dr. Richards admonished the people to keep the peace, stating that he had pledged his honor, and his life for their good conduct, when the people with one united voice resolved to trust to the law for a remedy of such a high-handed assassination, and when that failed, to call upon God to avenge them of their wrongs" (HC 6:626). Compare Willard Richards's note from Carthage, written on the day of the martyrdom: "The citizens here [Carthage] are afraid of the 'Mormons' attacking them; I promise them no" (HC 7:110).

31. See Oaks and Hill, *Carthage Conspiracy: The Trial of the Accused Assassins of Joseph Smith.*

32. See Corrill, *Brief History of the Church of Christ of Latter Day Saints,* p. 30.

33. McLellin plundered the house of jewelry and bed clothes. "Sister Emma cried and said that they had taken all of her bed clothes, except one quilt and blanket, and what could she do?" (See "Autobiography of John Lowe Butler," p. 16.)

34. HC 3:420.

35. See affidavit of Hyrum Smith in HC 3:404–24.

36. See D&C 121 and 122.

37. D&C 121:23.

38. D&C 122:8.

39. Joseph was aware of transgressions among the Saints that had incurred divine displeasure. He spoke specifically against profiteering and land speculation, and had warned them: "You say I am a Prophet. Well, then, I will prophesy, and when you go home write it down and remember it. You think you have been badly treated by your enemies; but if you don't do better than you are now doing, I prophesy that the state of Missouri will not hold you. Your sufferings have hardly commenced." (See recollection of David Osborne in JI 27 [March 15, 1892]: 173.)

40. Innocent children, for example, were wounded, killed, dragged into the snow, and mutilated. A company of Saints camped nearby received word of the massacre and of the mob's intention to attack them also. "Upon hearing this, some of the women picked up their babes and tried to wade through the deep snow, towards the neighboring woods, but after suffering almost beyond description from cold and exposure they were obliged to return to the wagons and trust in God for protection." (See Jenson, *Biographical Encyclopedia* 1:808–9; recollections of Lucy Walker Kimball in Walker and Stevenson, comps., *Ancestry and Descendants of John Walker*, pp. 27–28.)

41. Journal of Levi Richards, p. 88.

42. Statement of Joseph Millett, Sr., a son of Artemus Millett. See Millet, *Ancestors and Descendants of Thomas Millett. . . .*

43. *Lydia Knight's History*, pp. 11–12, 21–23.

44. See D&C 122:6. Willard Richards later recorded that Joseph said that he "was taken prisoner of war at Far West in his own door yard" and that his little boy clung to his garments. A man with a sword, blaspheming and blustering, thrust the boy away and said, "Get away, you little rascal, or I will run you through." (See entry of December 30, 1842, in "President Joseph Smith's Journal," December 21, 1842 to March 10, 1843, kept by Willard Richards, p. 15.)

45. See Smith, *Writings*, pp. 17–19. "Oh, God, seal our testimony to their hearts. Amen" (*Writings*, p. 17). "The Lord is with us," he wrote one evening, "but have much anxiety about my family" (*Writings*, p. 18). See also "Joseph Smith's Missionary Journal," *New Era* 4 (February 1974): 33–36.

46. HC 2:345; HC 6:134.

47. D&C 24:9.

48. *TPJS*, p. 315.

49. *WJS*, p. 123.

50. *TPJS*, p. 228; *WJS*, p. 118.

51. *TPJS*, pp. 240–41; *WJS*, p. 123.

52. See "Biography of Jane E. Manning James. . . ." The two came on bleeding feet, over 800 miles, from Buffalo, New York, to Nauvoo. They were born free, but were accused and harassed as if they were fugitive slaves.

53. Emma and Joseph tried to adopt Jane Manning into their family. She said no "because I did not understand or know what it meant. They were always good and kind to me, but I did not know my own mind." ("Biography of Jane E. Manning James . . . ," p. 20.)

54. Recalled by Mary Frost Adams in *YWJ* 17 (December 1906): 538.

55. See Johnson, *My Life's Review*, p. 97; journal of John Pulsipher.

56. *MS* 7 (January 15, 1846): 23.

57. *TPJS*, p. 90.

58. Apparently he had faith in the faith of little children. One evening, Joseph saw through a slightly opened door a little boy kneeling and praying that Joseph would be safe, would be protected from his enemies. The Prophet turned to the guards and said, "Brethren, you may all go to bed and sleep soundly, for the Lord has heard that little boy's prayer, and no harm will befall us this night." (Diary of Oliver B. Huntington, vol. 2, pp. 167–68.)

59. *YWJ* 17 (December 1906): 548.

60. *HC* 5:440; journal of Wandle Mace, pp. 85–86.

61. Joseph later reported this incident to Willard Richards as follows: "Hinkle ordered a retreat. I rode through and ordered them to stand, 300 against 3,000. A truce came and [they] said, 'We want Clemenson and wife and. . . . We will protect them. We will massacre all the rest.' They refused to go. I said, 'Go tell the army to retreat in 5 minutes or we'll give them hell' and they ran." (See entry of December 30, 1842, in "President Joseph Smith's Journal," December 21, 1842 to March 10, 1843, kept by Willard Richards, p. 18.)

62. "I thought that was a pretty bold stand to take, as we only numbered about two hundred to their thirty-five hundred" (see *The Gospel Kingdom*, pp. 354–55).

63. See Oscar F. Hunter, "Bishop Edward Hunter," *IE* 5 (September 1902): 870.

64. D&C 128:22.

65. In his letter to the exiled Saints in Missouri in December 1833, Joseph wrote: "Now there are two things of which I am ignorant and the Lord will not show me . . . : Why God hath suffered so great calamity to come upon Zion . . . and again by what means he will return her back to her inheritance with songs of everlasting joy upon her head [see D&C

101:18]." Instead, "when I enquire concerning this subject, the voice of the Lord is, 'Be still, and know that I am God! All those who suffer for my name shall reign with me, and he that layeth down his life for my sake shall find it again.' " Joseph was aware of transgressions among the Saints that had incurred divine displeasure. But because the innocent suffered, he wrote, "It is with difficulty that I can keep from complaining and murmuring against this dispensation." (See *Writings*, pp. 308–9.)

66. See D&C 101:9–18.

67. See Stevenson, *Reminiscences of Joseph, the Prophet*, pp. 5–6; Andrus, *They Knew*, p. 85. *Foxe's Book of Martyrs* includes accounts of John Wycliffe, John Huss, William Tyndale, Robert Smith, the Albigenses and Waldenses, and "a godly woman" put to death under the reign of King Henry VIII.

68. D&C 122:9.

69. See HC 7:212; Smith, *History of Joseph Smith*, p. 248; recollection of Lucy Walker Kimball in Littlefield, *Reminiscences of Latter-day Saints*, p. 45. After the martyrdom, Mother Smith recalled that in Missouri she had received a promise "that in five years Joseph should have power over all his enemies. The time had elapsed and the promise was fulfilled." (*History of Joseph Smith*, p. 325.)

70. TS 5 (November 1, 1844): 698. Nine of the Twelve were present in this meeting. Absent were John E. Page, Lyman Wight, and William Smith. See diary of Oliver B. Huntington, vol. 2, p. 378.

71. To James A. Bennett, a journalist and politician in New York who was drawn to the Prophet's character, he wrote, "On my part, I am ready to be offered up a sacrifice in that way that can bring to pass the greatest benefit and good. . . ." (HC 5:159.) Explaining his running for the Presidency he said, "If I lose my life in a good cause I am willing to be sacrificed on the altar of virtue, righteousness and truth, in maintaining the laws and Constitution of the United States, if need be, for the general good of mankind" (*TPJS*, p. 332).

72. There were other wives at this point, Benjamin Johnson added, "yet Emma, the wife of his youth, to me, appeared the queen of his heart and of his home" (see *Benjamin F. Johnson Letter*, p. 4). Jesse N. Smith, for whom Joseph and Emma provided a home, said of Emma: "I knew that queenly woman, his wife, Emma Smith. I may say that I was greatly impressed with her personality. She was the fitting helpmate of such a man. I stood in awe of this lady far more than I did of the Prophet himself, be-

cause she was so considerate of the feelings of the children." (*Journal of Jesse Nathaniel Smith*, p. 454.)

73. The next day Jedediah M. Grant asked the Prophet why he had turned pale after the incident. Joseph explained by referring to the spirit of life or the "virtue," as in the incident of the Master and the woman who touched his garment recorded in Luke 8:43–48. (See *TPJS*, pp. 280–81.)

74. See Levi Hancock's account of Joseph Smith's statement as told to his son, Mosiah Hancock, and recollected in "Life Story of Mosiah Lyman Hancock," pp. 27–29.

75. See experiences of Edwin Rushton as related by his son in Andrus, *They Knew*, p. 171. Compare Brigham Young's remarks: "Joseph said to me, 'God will take care of my children when I am taken.' " President Young added: "They are in the hands of God, and when they make their appearance before this people, full of his power, there are none but what will say—'Amen! we are ready to receive you.' " (*JD* 8:69.) See also entry of October 9, 1856, in journal of Wilford Woodruff.

## Chapter 5. Joseph Smith and the Kirtland Temple

1. "Behold, I will reveal unto you the Priesthood, by the hand of Elijah the prophet, before the coming of the great and dreadful day of the Lord" (D&C 2:1). This section contains portions of Moroni's words to the Prophet on the night of September 21, 1823.

2. See D&C 13, given on May 15, 1829. The sons of Levi anciently attended to the temple sacrifice, presumably offering it latterly in unrighteousness. In the last days they shall offer it in righteousness in a restored temple.

3. See Joseph Smith—History 1, p. 59, footnote.

4. See D&C 128, where the offering includes the presenting of accurate records. Compare D&C 124:37–39, where "your memorials for your sacrifices by the sons of Levi" are included as part of the order to be performed "in a house which you have built to my name."

5. See D&C 94, given on May 6, 1833. An earlier admonition about the house of the Lord to be built was given on December 27, 1832 (see D&C 88:119). The dimensions were not spelled out until the following May.

6. *JI* 27 (January 1, 1892): 23. See historical headnote to D&C 50.

7. *TPJS*, p. 204; *HC* 4:572. This is from an editorial ascribed to Joseph Smith appearing under the title, "Try the Spirits."

8. Speaking of "fallings, twitchings, swoonings, shaking, and trances," Joseph wrote, "Now God never had any prophets that acted in this way; there was nothing indecorous in the proceeding of the Lord's prophets in any age; neither had the apostles nor prophets in the apostles' day anything of this kind" (*TPJS*, p. 209). Compare Mother Smith's account of Joseph's comments: "When a man speaks by the Spirit of God, he speaks from the abundance of his heart—his mind is filled with intelligence, and even should he be excited, it does not cause him to do anything ridiculous or unseemly" (*History of Joseph Smith*, pp. 193–94).

9. *HC* 1:349.

10. D&C 95:3.

11. D&C 95:11.

12. D&C 95:12.

13. D&C 88:40 teaches that as intelligence cleaves to intelligence, and virtue to virtue, so does light to light. And surely love begets love.

14. *The Holy Temple*, p. 129. For an early reckoning of costs, see *MA* 1 (July 1835): 147–48; *MS* 14 (September 4, 1852): 438; *Contributor* 13 (April 1892): 251.

15. George A. Smith says that "they carried pistols about 3 in. long." Sometimes they were stoned. See Jenson, *Historical Record*, 1872–79; also *HC* 2:2. "We were obliged to keep up night watches to prevent being mobbed" (journal of Joel Hills Johnson, entry of September 23, 1835).

16. See journal of Truman O. Angell.

17. See discourse of Brigham Young in *JD* 1:133–35; Jenson, *Historical Record* 5:75.

18. See Nibley, *The Message of the Joseph Smith Papyri: An Egyptian Endowment*, p. 154.

19. On laying the first cornerstone at the "south-east corner" in harmony with the "strict order of the Priesthood," see *HC* 4:331. See also Joseph's use of the phrase, "Jesus Christ being the chief cornerstone," in his letter to Isaac Galland, March 22, 1839 (*Writings*, p. 418).

20. See Mary Elizabeth Rollins Lightner, in *Utah Genealogical and Historical Magazine* 17 (July 1926): 193–95; Andrus, *They Knew*, pp. 22–23.

21. See Mary Elizabeth Rollins Lightner Papers; *YWJ* 16 (December 1905): 556–57; Andrus, *They Knew*, pp. 23–24.

22. See her remarks at age eighty-seven at Brigham Young University.

23. See *Utah Genealogical and Historical Magazine* 28 (1937): 61; Snow, *Eliza R. Snow, an Immortal*, pp. 60–64.

24. See Zera Pulsipher papers.

25. See chapter five, note 57 herein.

26. See statement of Daniel Tyler, citing D&C 124, 1878, Church Archives, The Church of Jesus Christ of Latter-day Saints, Salt Lake City, Utah; also *JI* 15 (May 15, 1880): 111–12.

27. See the discourses of Joseph Smith in August, 1843, and notes, in *WJS*, pp. 236–48, 300–308.

28. The official history says "probably five or six" hundred "assembled before the doors were opened." An overflow meeting was held in a nearby schoolhouse. Even then "many were left out." (*HC* 2:410–11.) Later dedicatory services were held to accommodate the many others.

29. See Jillaine K. Baker, "The Dedication of the Kirtland Temple," typescript.

30. See, for example, the meeting on Thursday, January 14, 1836, where "rules and regulations to be observed in the 'House of the Lord' " were drafted, all to enhance the order, dignity, and worship in the building (*HC* 2:368).

31. See D&C 88.

32. See George A. Smith's comments in *JD* 2:215.

33. D&C 88:74, 123–26. See also D&C 38:42; 133:5. Following such a course of sanctification can prepare us to eventually become the very vessels of the Lord. Section 93, for instance, teaches that we may "receive a fulness" through worship—a fulness of truth, of light, and of glory (D&C 93:9–20).

34. *TPJS*, p. 92; *HC* 2:310.

35. *HC* 2:410; compare Archibald F. Bennett, "The Kirtland Temple," *Utah Genealogical and Historical Magazine* 27 (1936): 86.

36. *HC* 2:413–16.

37. *HC* 2:416.

38. D&C 109:78–79.

39. This shout, Joseph said, "sealed the proceedings of the day" (HC 2:427).

40. The Saints are commanded to bless the name of the Lord with "loud" voices and "with a sound of rejoicing" by Hosanna—see D&C 19:37; 36:3; 39:19; 124:101. At times in the Kirtland Temple they also used an expression from 3 Nephi, "Blessed be the name of the Most High God!" (3 Nephi 11:17; see also D&C 39:19.) Joseph records going home after a night of praise and blessing in the Kirtland Temple, and "my soul cried hosanna to God and the Lamb, through the silent watches of the night" (HC 2:387).

41. See Journal History, October 1909; Snow, *Eliza R. Snow, an Immortal*, p. 62.

42. The histories make no mention of a benediction either in the morning or the afternoon session. Perhaps the Saints did not consider the meetings closed, since they returned for further meetings. See Jillaine K. Baker, "The Dedication of the Kirtland Temple," p. 14.

43. Daniel Tyler wrote of this period of dedication: "All felt that they had a foretaste of heaven. In fact, there were several weeks in which we were not tempted of the devil; and we wondered whether the millennium had commenced. At or near the close of the endowments, the Prophet Joseph . . . said: 'Brethren, for some time Satan has not had power to tempt you. Some have thought that there would be no more temptation. But the opposite will come; and unless you draw near to the Lord, you will be overcome and apostatize.' " (As found in *Scraps of Biography*, pp. 32–33.)

44. Erastus Snow, for one, records: "In the evening they ate the passover and feasted upon bread and wine until they were filled, and after these things were over the disciples went from house to house breaking bread and eating it with joyful hearts, being filled with the spirit of prophecy; and the sick were healed and Devils were cast out" (journal of Erastus Snow, 1836, p. 8).

45. See recollection of Prescindia Huntington in Tullidge, *The Women of Mormondom*, p. 207. Joseph describes an earlier meeting where "the gift of tongues fell upon us in mighty power, angels mingled their voices with ours, while their presence was in our midst, and unceasing praises swelled our bosoms for the space of half an hour" (see entry of January 22, 1836, in diary of Joseph Smith, 1835–36, p. 141; *Writings*, pp. 148–49).

46. Of the evening of the dedication day, when the Prophet met with the priesthood quorums and another great outpouring of the Spirit took place, it is recorded: "The people of the neighborhood came running together (hearing an unusual sound within, and seeing a bright light like a pillar of fire resting upon the temple) and were astonished at what was taking place. This continued until the meeting closed at 11:00 p.m." (HC 2:428.)

47. This is John Taylor's recollection. See *JD* 24:197.

48. See *HC* 2:387–92, 430–33. Jeremiah Willey records: "Joseph Smith requested the Elders to speak their feelings freely and sing, exhort and pray as the Spirit should give utterance. The meeting continued the whole night. Many of the gifts were poured out upon the people; at break of day we were dismissed." (Autobiography of Jeremiah Willey, pp. 10–12.)

49. Zina D. Huntington and her sister Prescindia "both heard, from one corner of the room above our heads, a choir of angels singing most beautifully. They were invisible to us, but myriads of angelic voices seemed to be united in singing some song of Zion, and their sweet harmony filled the temple of God." (See Tullidge, *Women of Mormondom*, p. 207–8.)

50. Prescindia Huntington recalled: "Brother McCarter rose and sang a song of Zion in tongues; I arose and sang simultaneously with him the same tune and words, beginning and ending each verse in perfect unison, without varying a word. It was just as though we had sung it together a thousand times." (As cited in Tullidge, *Women of Mormondom*, pp. 208–9.)

51. D&C 76:94; 84:98.

52. George A. Smith recalled that some felt "too little" and some "too much" (*JD* 2:215).

53. As cited in Whitney, *Life of Heber C. Kimball*, pp. 91, 92.

54. "When the afternoon meeting assembled, Joseph, feeling very much elated, arose the first thing and said the personage who had appeared in the morning was the Angel Peter come to accept the dedication" (journal of Truman O. Angell, p. 5).

55. *Eliza R. Snow, an Immortal*, p. 62.

56. HC 2:428. The Prophet records the seeing of angels. Others who left records in their journals include Brigham Young, Joel H. Johnson,

and Erastus Snow. Among the women who recorded these events were Eliza R. Snow and Prescindia Huntington. See, for example, Brigham Young in S. Dilworth Young, *"Here Is Brigham . . .,"* p. 143.

57. *YWJ* 8 (February 1897): 240. Joseph and his father had made the same request—the former in the dedicatory prayer (see D&C 109:36-37). Oliver Cowdery wrote under date of March 27, 1836, which was Sunday, the day of dedication: "In the evening I met with the officers of the church in the Lord's house. The Spirit was poured out—I saw the glory of God, like a great cloud, come down and rest upon the house, and fill the same like a mighty rushing wind." There were 316 present for this meeting. (See Leonard J. Arrington, ed., "Oliver Cowdery's Kirtland, Ohio, 'Sketch Book,' " p. 426.)

58. See Sampson and Wimmer, "The Kirtland Safety Society: The Stock Ledger Book and the Bank Failure," pp. 427-36; Partridge, "The Failure of the Kirtland Safety Society," pp. 437-54.

59. Sampson and Wimmer, "Stock Ledger Book," p. 436.

60. See Backman, *The Heavens Resound*, p. 318.

61. Journal of Truman O. Angell.

62. See Backman, *The Heavens Resound*, pp. 368-72; McGavin, "The Kirtland Temple Defiled," pp. 594-95.

63. *HC* 2:435; historical headnote to D&C 110.

64. D&C 110:1-3.

65. See Proclamation of the Twelve, 1845, in Clark, ed., *Messages of the First Presidency of The Church of Jesus Christ of Latter-day Saints* 1:258.

66. D&C 110:4.

67. *TPJS*, p. 92. Three years earlier Joseph had written the following to W. W. Phelps on January 11, 1833: "We greatly fear before the Lord lest we should fail of this great honor which our Master proposes to confer on us; we are seeking for humility and great faith lest we be ashamed in his presence" (*Writings*, p. 263).

68. D&C 110:7, 10.

69. D&C 110:11-12.

70. D&C 110:13-16.

## Chapter 6. Joseph Smith as Teacher, Speaker, and Counselor

1. D&C 88:122-38.

2. D&C 88:138. To become "clean" in this sense required an ordinance. It was also interpreted to require carrying the gospel abroad (see journal of Jonathan H. Hale, p. 27). One purpose of the washing of feet, Joseph explained, was "to unite our hearts, that we may be one in feeling and sentiment" (*TPJS*, p. 91). In addition there are sacred instructions that "after partaking of bread and wine" the President of the Church is to gird himself and wash the feet of his brethren (D&C 88:140-41). Mother Smith recorded the following: "At this time [when] my sons were all called home [from missions] . . . Joseph took all the male portion of our family into the . . . schoolroom and administered to them the ordinance of washing of feet; after which the Spirit fell upon them, and they spake in tongues, and prophesied. . . . At that time I was on the farm a short distance from the place where the meeting was held, and my children being anxious that I should enjoy the meeting, sent a messenger in great haste for me. I went without delay, and shared with the rest, the most glorious out-pouring of the Spirit of God that had ever before taken place in the Church. We felt that we had gained a decided victory over the adversary." (*History of Joseph Smith*, p. 224.)

3. "Being born again," Joseph told the Twelve, "comes by the Spirit of God through ordinances" (*TPJS*, p. 162; *WJS*, p. 12).

4. D&C 88:122.

5. D&C 88:133.

6. "I say unto you, my friends. . . ." (D&C 88:117; see also 93:51; 94:1; 100:1.) Joseph referred to this designation as a privilege: in his dedicatory prayer at the Kirtland Temple he spoke gratefully of "a revelation . . . calling us thy friends" (see D&C 109:6).

7. *TPJS*, p. 24.

8. D&C 63:61, 64, 66.

9. *TPJS*, p. 69.

10. Once the Prophet was pacing back and forth in the hallway of his home. Two of his sons were imitating him, trying to take steps as long as his, and often stumbling and scuffling. The peals of laughter from the other children who were watching were accompanied by the two boys'

squeaky shoes. The Prophet was apparently unaware, or in any case unperturbed. (See reported recollection of Adeline Hatch Barber in *YWJ* 28 [December 1917]: 656.)

11. D&C 100:7–8.

12. D&C 84:85.

13. *TPJS*, p. 320. This statement was made at the funeral of Judge Higbee.

14. See *WJS*, p. 80; also Snow, "Sketch of My Life," *The Relief Society Magazine* 31 (March 1944): 136.

15. Recounted to the author by Elder Hugh B. Brown, whose wife, Zina, was a granddaughter of Brigham Young. See *New Era* 6 (April 1976): 16.

16. John 15:5.

17. D&C 50:16–24.

18. Said in conversation with the author.

19. D&C 11:21.

20. See discourse of Jedediah M. Grant in *JD* 3:67.

21. *JD* 8:206.

22. *TPJS*, p. 162; *WJS*, p. 12.

23. D&C 1:24.

24. As cited in Journal History, February 19, 1837. "His deportment is calm and dignified . . . no ostentation, no affectation of address or manners" (journal of William I. Appleby, 1841).

25. *YWJ* 16 (December 1905): 556.

26. *YWJ* 16 (December 1905): 558.

27. See McGavin, *Nauvoo the Beautiful*, pp. 81–82.

28. *YWJ* 2 (September 1891): 574.

29. "Joseph Smith a True Prophet," *YWJ* 31 (April 1920): 212. Elizabeth H. B. Hyde recalled a meeting in the Grove on her first Sabbath in Nauvoo. "His words thrilled my whole being, and I knew he was a prophet of God." (*Utah Genealogical and Historical Magazine* 3 [1912]: 207.)

30. Journal of Alfred Cordon, 1841–44.

31. *YWJ* 17 (December 1906): 546.

32. P. 18.

33. John 3:5.

34. Luke 17:21; italics added.

35. "Except a man be born again he cannot *see* the kingdom of God; second, except a man be born of water and the Spirit he cannot *enter* into the kingdom of God" (*WJS*, p. 209; italics added).

36. See recollection of Daniel Tyler in *JI* 27 (February 1, 1892): 93-94.

37. Autobiography of Mary Louisa Woolley Clark, p. 1; Arrington, *From Quaker to Latter-day Saint: Bishop Edwin D. Woolley*, pp. 86-87; Jenson, *Biographical Encyclopedia* 1:631-32.

38. See D&C 132:51; HC 2:182; *TPJS*, p. 322; *WJS*, pp. 246, 372.

39. See the author's "Power from Abrahamic Tests," in *The Highest In Us*, p. 49.

40. "I told her also that we would never be separated" ("Last Sermon of Heber C. Kimball," p. 123).

41. See Helen Mar Whitney (daughter of Heber C. Kimball), "Scenes and Incidents in Nauvoo," p. 74.

42. *TPJS*, p. 258.

43. *TPJS*, p. 241.

44. *TPJS*, p. 364.

45. See reported recollection of Jesse W. Crosby in Cox, "Stories from Notebook," p. 2; Andrus, *They Knew*, p. 144.

46. See, for example, D&C 3:1-15; 20:5; 93:47; 132:60. He was reproved for having "gone on in the persuasions of men" and for having "suffered the counsel of [his] director to be trampled upon from the beginning" (D&C 3:6, 15). In section 20 the Lord speaks of Joseph's being "entangled again in the vanities of the world" (D&C 20:5), and then of his having repented and received commandments which "inspired him" (D&C 20:6-7). After the loss of the 116 manuscript pages, the Lord told Joseph: "Repent of that which thou hast done which is contrary to the commandment which I gave you, and thou art still chosen, and art again called to the work" (D&C 3:10).

47. "Brother Parley, God bless you, go your way rejoicing, preach the gospel, fill the measure of your mission, and walk such things under your feet" (*Autobiography of Parley P. Pratt*, p. 118).

48. See discourse of Brigham Young in *JD* 5:331.

49. See discourse of Brigham Young in *The Deseret News*, June 6, 1877, p. 274.

50. Quincy, *Figures of the Past*, p. 397.

## Chapter 7. Doctrinal Development and the Nauvoo Era

1. *WJS*, p. 418. The precise date of this sermon is not established. It is placed in Appendix B of *WJS*.

2. *HC* 5:1–2; *TPJS*, p. 237.

3. See discourse of John Taylor in *JD* 25:183.

4. D&C 124:42.

5. *TPJS*, p. 237.

6. See journal of L. John Nuttall, vol. 1, pp. 18–19.

7. *TPJS*, p. 237.

8. *TPJS*, p. 91; compare D&C 109:15.

9. *JI* 27 (June 1, 1892): 345. "In the fall of 1843, George A. and Bathsheba received their endowments and were united under the holy order of celestial marriage. . . . She met often with her husband, Joseph and others who had received their endowments, in an upper room dedicated for the purpose, and prayed with them repeatedly in those meetings." (Jenson, *Biographical Encyclopedia* 1:700.)

10. *JI* 27 (July 1, 1892): 400.

11. This is from an address given in April 1842. See *TPJS*, p. 224; *WJS*, p. 115. On May 4, 1844, Joseph met with the First Presidency, the Twelve, and the Temple Committee, to whom he said, "We need the temple more than anything else" (*HC* 6:230). William Clayton recorded that, in the context of a discussion of marriage and the covenant of marriage, "[Joseph] said that he could not reveal the fulness of these things until the temple is completed" (see *WJS*, p. 233, and footnote 11, pp. 293–94).

12. For example, Sarah Rich recorded: "Many were the blessings we had received in the house of the Lord [she and her husband labored in the temple from 7:00 a.m. until midnight each day for several weeks] which has caused us joy and comfort in the midst of all our sorrows and enabled us to have faith in God, knowing he would guide us and sustain

us in the unknown journey that lay before us. For if it had not been for the faith and knowledge that was bestowed upon us in that temple by the influence and help of the Spirit of the Lord, our journey would have been like one taking a leap in the dark." (Autobiography of Sarah DeArmon Pea Rich.)

13. See Little, *Jacob Hamblin*, p. 8.

14. See statement of Horace Cummings in Lundwall, comp., *The Vision*, p. 141.

15. Of this journal, B. H. Roberts wrote: "Men may found hospitals or temples or schools for the Church, or endow special divisions or chairs of learning in them; or they may make consecrations of lands and other property to the Church, but . . . no one will surpass in excellence and permanence or largeness the service [of] . . . the beautiful and splendid journals he [Wilford Woodruff] kept through sixty-three eventful years—so far do the things of mind surpass material things" (CHC 6:355).

16. D&C 124:28-36. See also Wilford Woodruff, in *The Deseret News Weekly* 42 (April 25, 1891): 554.

17. Sariah Robbins Pulsipher recalled that "all the inhabitants [of Nauvoo] met on the banks of the Mississippi River, just behind the Smith house, for the purpose of baptizing for the dead" (see reported recollection of Sariah Robbins Pulsipher in *YWJ* 17 [December 1906]: 545). James Phippen said that he "saw the Prophet and others baptize 600 one day in the Mississippi River" (*YWJ* 17 [December 1906]: 540).

18. See Wilford Woodruff, in *The Deseret News Weekly* 42 (April 25, 1891): 554. See also D&C 128; *WJS*, p. 368.

19. Diary of William Holmes Walker, pp. 7-14; Andrus, *They Knew*, p. 148.

20. See Quincy, *Figures of the Past*, pp. 336-40.

21. See Adams, "Charles Francis Adams Visits the Mormons in 1844," p. 285.

22. Journal History, April 9, 1837; Cowley, *Wilford Woodruff*, p. 68.

23. See journal of Wandle Mace, p. 168.

24. "The precious instructions which I received in the councils of the church during that winter and spring were indeed more than all I had learned before in my life" (journal of Erastus Snow, 1841-47, p. 96).

25. Parley P. Pratt, in a proclamation to the Church dated January 1, 1845, quoted the Prophet as follows: "I know not why; but for some

reason I am constrained to hasten my preparations, and to confer upon the Twelve all the ordinances, keys, covenants, endowments, and sealing ordinances of the priesthood, and so set before them a pattern in all things pertaining to the sanctuary and the endowment therein" (MS 5 [March 1845]: 151). Wilford Woodruff wrote on October 11, 1844: "Addressing the Twelve, [Joseph] exclaimed, 'Upon your shoulders the kingdom rests, and you must round up your shoulders, and bear it; for I have had to do it until now. But now the responsibility rests upon you.' " (TS 5 [November 1, 1844]: 698.) Years later Wilford Woodruff said: "The Prophet Joseph Smith called the Apostles together and he delivered unto them the ordinances of the church and kingdom of God, and all the keys and powers that God had bestowed upon him, he sealed upon our heads, and he told us we must round up our shoulders and bear off this kingdom, or we would be damned" (see entry of September 13, 1883, in journal of Wilford Woodruff; also *The Discourses of Wilford Woodruff*, p. 72).

26. Parley P. Pratt wrote: "He proceeded to confer on elder Young, the President of the Twelve, the keys of the sealing power, as conferred in the last days by the spirit and power of Elijah. . . . This last key of the priesthood is the most sacred of all, and pertains exclusively to the first presidency of the Church." (MS 5 [March 1845]: 151.)

27. See Appendix 4 in Roberts, *Rise and Fall*, p. 416.

28. See, for example, HC 5:23; also *Woman's Exponent* 9 (November 12, 1880): 102.

29. See, for example, TPJS, p. 238, where the Prophet speaks of woman's "refined feelings and sensitiveness." Compare TPJS, pp. 229, 241.

30. Joseph told the newly-created society that the designation of Emma Smith as "elect lady" in this revelation (D&C 25:3) is similar to the use of that title in 2 John 1:1, and he said it meant that she was "elected to preside." He explained that "she was ordained at the time the revelation was given [July 1830] to expound the scriptures to all and to teach the female part of the community; and that not she alone, but others, may attain to the same blessings." (See WJS, p. 105.)

31. President Emma Smith said to the society: "We are going to do something extraordinary. When a boat is stuck in the rapids, with a multitude of 'Mormons' on board, we shall consider that a loud call for relief. We expect extraordinary occasions and pressing calls." (See Minute book

for Nauvoo Relief Society, kept by Eliza R. Snow, March 17, 1842 to March 16, 1844.)

32. "I ask what right has any man, or set of men, or priest, or set of priests, to say if a man will not do so and so he shall be damned. Is he not taking upon himself or assuming the character of a prophet? Consequently he must either be a true or false prophet." (*WJS*, p. 230; see also *WJS*, p. 345.)

33. "So many of our enemies said now Mormonism was at an end and we would all be scattered to the four winds, but our faith never failed" (autobiography of Sarah DeArmon Pea Rich, pp. 63–64).

34. *HC* 5:540; *WJS*, p. 218. See original in *TS* 3 (March 1, 1842): 709.

35. After Joseph Smith had heard Heber C. Kimball relate his encounter with evil spirits as the brethren opened the mission in Britain, Heber asked if there was anything wrong with him that he should have been so assaulted. Joseph related some of his own struggles with evil powers and said, "The nearer a person approaches the Lord, a greater power will be manifested by the adversary to prevent the accomplishment of His purposes" (as cited in Whitney, *Life of Heber C. Kimball*, p. 132). This is a principle he extended to all forms of progress for mankind, whether intellectual, scientific, cultural, or social. "It is the same," he remarked elsewhere, "with men whom God inspires to make inventions, improvements and discoveries for the improvement of man generally. . . . They will be opposed and persecuted by the ones their works are designed to benefit and bless." (Recollection of O.B. Huntington in *YWJ* [April 1893]: 321.)

36. In a letter to James Arlington Bennett in New York, September 8, 1842, *HC* 5:156.

37. "Let us teach the things of Jesus Christ" (*HC* 6:411). "I have set your minds at liberty by letting you know the things of Christ Jesus" (*HC* 6:412).

38. *HC* 4:42.

39. Diary of Charles L. Walker, p. 902.

40. Recalled by Milo Andrus, who heard Joseph say this in Nauvoo. See Joseph Smith papers.

41. Recollections of Howard Coray in record of the Utah Stake of Zion, June 11, 1871.

42. *WJS*, p. 162. See also recollection of Elston Kelsey in Walker, comp., "Sayings of the Prophet Joseph."

43. See *TPJS*, p. 366. Heber C. Kimball likewise recalled the Prophet saying that a coward could not be saved in the kingdom of God (see Whitney, *Life of Heber C. Kimball*, p. 323).

44. Recollection of James Hood, oral tradition. Earlier the Prophet remarked, "We will never be justly charged with the sin of ingratitude" (*HC* 4:480). See also *WJS*, p. 178, where the context suggests it is better to lose money than "be guilty of the sin of ingratitude." See also George Q. Cannon, *Life of Joseph Smith the Prophet*, p. 527.

45. D&C 78:19.

46. *TPJS*, p. 364.

47. Recollection of Oliver B. Huntington in *YWJ* 2 (May 1891): 366; Andrus, *They Knew*, p. 61. Joseph elsewhere said, "It is a false principle for a man to aggrandize himself at the expense of another." And he added, "Everything God does is to aggrandize His kingdom." (*HC* 5:285.) Compare *WJS*, p. 165.

48. Mark 8:35. The JST of Mark 8:37–38 clarifies: "For whosoever will save his life, shall lose it; or whosoever will save his life, shall be willing to lay it down for my sake; and if he is not willing to lay it down for my sake, he shall lose it. But whosoever shall be willing to lose his life for my sake, and the gospel, the same shall save it." Compare JST Matthew 16:26–27.

49. Mark 8:36. See also Matthew 16:26; Luke 9:25.

50. See this report of President Snow under entry of January 1, 1892, in diary of Abraham H. Cannon, vol. 16, p. 30.

51. "The Prophet said to me [Brigham Young] about sixteen years ago [at Kirtland], 'If I was to show the Latter-day Saints all the revelations that the Lord has shown unto me, there is scarce a man that would stay with me, they could not bear it'" (*MS* 13 [September 1, 1851]: 257).

52. *HC* 2:477. Compare George Q. Cannon, in Conference Report, April 6, 1900, p. 57.

53. As recalled by Parley P. Pratt in *MS* 55 (September 4, 1893): 585.

54. See diary of George Laub, pp. 11–12.

55. In the Joseph Smith Translation, John the Baptist says, "I am not that Elias who was to restore all things. And they asked him, saying, Art thou that Prophet? And he answered, No." (JST, John 1:22.) John, it ap-

pears, was a forerunner, and in that sense an Elias. But he was not, in his own eyes, "that Elias who was to restore all things."

56. Some scholars conclude that all these strands of prophecy were embodied and fulfilled in Christ; others conclude that each sect or group had its own peculiar version of the messianic hope; while some believe that the Redemptive Messiah, the Preparing Messiah, and the Priestly Messiah are three different persons. In fact, the elaboration of messianic expectation and the overlay of fancy, tradition, and speculation means that today both Judaism and Christianity are multi-messianic. The restoration is mono-messianic. It appears that there is one and only one who deserves the title.

57. Acts 3:20–26.

58. See diary of George Laub, pp. 11–12. Joseph repeatedly rebuked Martin Harris for trying to apply Old Testament prophecies to him (Joseph) that did not apply. Such a course, he told Brigham Young, would destroy the kingdom of God. (JD 2:127.) "Are you the Savior?" he was once asked. "No," he replied, "but I can tell you what I am—I am his brother." (See recollection of Brigham Young in JD 14:202.) There is nothing in his teaching that ascribes the glory of the Messianic role to himself or to anyone else except to Christ himself.

59. WJS, p. 370; diary of George Laub, p. 12. According to Laub, Joseph's paraphrase of John 1 was as follows: "The Jews asked John the Baptist if he was Elias or Jesus or that great prophet that was to come." Laub did not transcribe into his journal the notes on this discourse until about a year after it was given. See WJS, p. 405, note 50.

60. HC 6:346.

61. TPJS, p. 365.

62. See "A Family Meeting in Nauvoo: Minutes of a meeting of the Richards and Young Families held in Nauvoo, Ill., Jan. 8, 1845," Utah Genealogical and Historical Magazine 11 (July 1920): 104–17.

63. Genesis 49:22–26; 2 Nephi 3:6–15. See statements collected in Our Lineage, a 1933 lesson manual for genealogy classes.

64. See 1853 letter from Orson to Parley P. Pratt.

65. See Church News, December 23, 1984, p. 14. Lathrop lived from 1584–1653. See John Lathrop: Reformer, Sufferer, Pilgrim, Man of God; Bennett, "The Ancestry of Joseph Smith the Prophet," pp. 66–69; Bennett, Saviors on Mount Zion, pp. 85–90. In 1859 Brigham Young stated: "Joseph Smith, Junior, was foreordained to come through the loins of Abraham,

Isaac, Jacob, Joseph, and so on down through the Prophets and Apostles; and thus he came forth in the last days to be a minister of salvation, and to hold the keys of the last dispensation of the fulness of times" (*JD* 7:289–90).

66. See *TPJS*, pp. 149–50.

## Chapter 8. The Last Months and Martyrdom

1. Journal of Mary Elizabeth Rollins Lightner, p. 7.

2. Hebrews 9:16–17.

3. *JD* 18:361. Mother Smith recollected that when he was leaving Kirtland for Missouri, Joseph said in a council meeting: "One thing, brethren is certain, I shall see you again, let what will happen, for I have a promise of life five years, and they cannot kill me until that time is expired" (*History of Joseph Smith*, p. 248). On July 28, 1844, Wilford Woodruff recorded Lyman Wight saying that while they were in Liberty Jail in 1839 Joseph told him that he (Joseph) would not live to see forty years, but that he was not to speak of it until Joseph was dead (excerpt from Wilford Woodruff's journal in *HC* 7:212). Mother Smith remembered also that in Missouri she received a promise "that in five years Joseph should have power over all his enemies." She did not anticipate his premature death. But when it occurred she wrote: "The time had elapsed and the promise was fulfilled." (*History of Joseph Smith*, p. 325.) Lucy Walker quoted him, "I have the promise of life for five years, if I listen to the voice of the Spirit." But she said this was in June 1844, just before Joseph crossed the river to Montrose. Was this a promise of five *more* years? Or a slip of memory on the time of the statement? Or did she misunderstand? (See sketch of Lucy Walker in Walker and Stevenson, comps., *Ancestry and Descendants of John Walker*, p. 31.)

4. *JD* 3:364.

5. See Cowley, *Wilford Woodruff*, pp. 204–5.

6. *TPJS*, p. 216; *WJS*, p. 112.

7. John Bushman wrote: "The Prophet Joseph and his brother Hyrum were fond of visiting or calling on the saints in their homes. In this way the people became more intimately acquainted with them and loved them for the great interest they took in the people. The leaders were very anxious to have the work on the Temple pushed to comple-

tion." (*John Bushman: Utah-Arizona Pioneer 1843-1926*, p. 6.) William Adams recalled how the Prophet worked with the men and encouraged them "not to slacken their hands," and asked the Saints to pay their tithing faithfully (diary of William Adams, p. 11). On March 7, 1844, Joseph announced, "We can put the roof on this building this season. By turning all the means of the Nauvoo House and doubling our diligence, we can do it." (*WJS*, p. 322.)

    8. See *HC* 6:236; 250-52; 363-65.

    9. *HC* 6:298. The First Presidency had issued a call for the building of the Nauvoo Temple in April 1841, saying that "on its speedy erection great blessings depend" (*HC* 4:339). This was repeated in later settings. See, for example, Hyrum Smith's remarks on March 7, 1844: "The object of the meeting is to stir up your minds by way of remembrance. It is necessary to have a starting-point, which is to build the Temple. . . . Much depends upon it for our endowments and sealing powers; and many blessings depend upon it." (*HC* 6:236-37.) In a conference talk on April 6, 1844, Hyrum said: "I cannot make a comparison between the House of God and anything now in existence. Great things are to grow out of that house. There is a great and mighty power to grow out of it. There is an endowment. Knowledge is power. We want knowledge. . . . We are now deprived of the privilege of giving the necessary instruction; hence we want a house." (*HC* 6:298-99.)

    10. See journal of John Pulsipher, p. 6.

    11. See, for example, this entry: "I rode with Emma to the Temple for the benefit of her health" (*HC* 5:182). "I would to God that this temple was now done, that we might go into it and go to work, and improve our time, and make use of the seals while they are on earth" (*WJS*, p. 318). "My only trouble at the present time is concerning ourselves, that the Saints will be divided, broken up, and scattered, before we get our salvation secure" (*TPJS*, p. 331; *WJS*, p. 319).

    12. Joseph had a total of twenty-six scribes at different times. Several failed him. "There are but few subjects that I have felt a greater anxiety about than my history, which has been a very difficult task, on account of the death of my best clerks [Robert B. Thompson, for example] and the apostasy of others [Oliver Cowdery, Warren Parrish] and the stealing of records by John Whitmer, Cyrus Smalling and others" (*HC* 6:66). Among the able record keepers at Nauvoo were William W. Phelps, James Sloan, William Clayton, Wilford Woodruff, and Willard Richards. On January 20, 1843, the Prophet gave instructions to William W. Phelps

and Willard Richards about "uniting in writing the history of the church" ("President Joseph Smith's Journal," kept by Willard Richards, p. 140). The background of loss and interruption gives greater weight to Joseph's comment on Richards. "I have been searching all my life to find a man after my own heart, whom I could trust with my business in all things, and I have found him. Dr. Willard Richards is the man." (Journal History, November 21, 1841.) Richards was one of the two members of the Twelve he did not send away in the final weeks of his life. To him and John Taylor we are indebted for the most careful records of those final weeks.

13. *HC* 5:394.

14. *HC* 2:199. About this irretrievable loss he expressed deep sorrow in the Kirtland days, saying that if minutes had been kept, they "would decide almost every point of doctrine which might be agitated." Further, because of this neglect, he said, "We cannot bear record to the Church and to the world, of the great and glorious manifestations which have been made to us with that degree of power and authority we otherwise could." (*HC* 2:199; *TPJS*, p. 72.)

15. Wilford Woodruff recorded this meeting shortly after. Others wrote their summaries later. See, for example, letter of Orson Hyde to John S. Fullmer, September 27, 1844. Also Elder Orson Hyde said: "We were in council with Brother Joseph almost every day for weeks. Says Brother Joseph in one of these councils, there is something going to happen; I don't know what it is, but the Lord bids me to hasten and give you your endowment before the temple is finished. He conducted us through every ordinance of the holy priesthood, and when he had gone through with all the ordinances he rejoiced very much, and says, now if they kill me you have got all the keys, and all the ordinances and you can confer them upon others, and the hosts of Satan will not be able to tear down the kingdom, as fast as you will be able to build it up; and now, says he, on your shoulders will be the responsibility of leading this people right, for the Lord is going to let me rest a while." (As cited in Grant, *A Collection of Facts, Relative to the Course Taken by Elder Sidney Rigdon . . .* , pp. 24–25.)

16. See Journal History, March 12, 1897. This is a late statement—fifty-three years later—of Wilford Woodruff, who added in this letter to Elder Heber J. Grant that Joseph's charge was still "ringing in my ears."

17. See Benjamin F. Johnson's testimony regarding these matters in *The Benjamin F. Johnson Letter*, pp. 10–11, 21–22.

18. Journal of Wandle Mace, p. 168.

19. *JD* 13:164.

20. Three trusted men "fitted out" the room in "the upper part of the brick store." "He [Joseph] told us that the object he had for us was to go to work and fit up that room preparatory to giving endowments to a few Elders, that he might give unto them all the keys of power pertaining to the Aaronic and Melchisedec Priesthoods." (See affidavit of Lucius N. Scovil, Dimick B. Huntington, and Shadrack Roundy in *The Deseret News*, February 15, 1884.)

21. See diary of Reuben McBride. The font had been dedicated on November 8, 1841. See journal of William Clayton.

22. Dissention was already at work. In his last discourse in the Grove, given on June 16, 1844, he said this was a purging process. "I have reason to think that the Church is being purged" (*WJS*, p. 380).

23. Even on the next to last day of their lives, June 26, "Hyrum encouraged Joseph to think that the Lord, for his Church's sake, would release him from prison" (*HC* 6:592).

24. See John Taylor's description of the fomenting forces in Appendix 4 of Roberts, *Rise and Fall*.

25. See Joseph W. McMurrin's report of his interview with Richard S. Law in *IE* 6 (May 1903): 507–10.

26. Brigham Young and Joseph F. Smith, among others, assert that the Prophet understood as early as 1831 that the principle of plural marriage would be reestablished in modern times. See Journal History, February 17, 1882; *The Deseret News*, February 17, 1882; Widtsoe, *Joseph Smith*, p. 237.

27. According to a recollection of Brigham Young, unpublished discourse of October 8, 1866, Church Archives, The Church of Jesus Christ of Latter-day Saints, Salt Lake City, Utah.

28. The Laws and Robert D. Foster were excommunicated in April 1844. A few days later they organized their own church, making Law its president. They had been holding secret meetings that plotted against the Prophet since March of 1844. See *HC* 6:341, 347.

29. See in D&C 124:88–107 the extent and dignity of William Law's standing in 1841. It is an irony that he was called in January of that year to declare the gospel "with great joy, as he shall be moved upon by my Spirit, unto the inhabitants of Warsaw, and also unto the inhabitants of Carthage," yet within three years he was a primary factor in the lethal op-

position that was generated in those two Illinois communities. Apparently the excommunication and the public denunciation of Law and others were factors in their violent spirit of revenge. See, for example, journal of James Palmer, p. 78.

30. See Prospectus, May 10, 1844, and *Expositor*, pp. 1, 3.

31. Precedents for this would continue to build up until the turn of the century. The deliberations of the city council were lengthy, and they anticipated some of the consequences of the action finally taken. Yet William Clayton calls the *Expositor* the "engine of destruction" (journal of William Clayton).

32. See Oaks and Hill, *Carthage Conspiracy*.

33. Diary of George Laub, p. 18.

34. HC 6:433.

35. See diary of Joseph Fielding, vol. 5, p. 38; also HC 6:451, 503, 505, 506-52.

36. On June 20 Joseph forwarded to President John Tyler in Washington, D.C., the affidavits that spelled out the swirl of forces and the threats of "utter extermination" from both Missouri and Illinois. He appealed to the President of the United States to render "that protection which the Constitution guarantees in case of 'insurrection and rebellion.'" Nothing was done in response. See HC 6:508.

37. On a charge of riot Joseph and the city council were tried and acquitted by the justice of the peace Daniel H. Wells. See HC 6:488-91.

38. Carthage was headquarters for "the caucus" who had threatened to destroy all the Smith family in a few weeks, including Joseph H. Jackson, Mike Barnes, Captain Singleton, and a Missourian who boasted of his murder of men, women, and children in Missouri. The Prophet assigned Daniel Carns to carry to Governor Ford this information, which was brought him by Gilbert Balnap. (See entry of March 24, 1844, in "President Joseph Smith's Journal," kept by Willard Richards, p. 48; WJS, pp. 337-38; HC 6:272.)

39. HC 6:536.

40. HC 6:567-68.

41. On the threats of Joseph H. Jackson, see the description by John Taylor in Appendix 4 of Roberts, *Rise and Fall*, p. 419. In his bitterness (he had wanted to marry a daughter of Hyrum Smith) Jackson said "a Smith should not be alive two weeks, not over two months anyhow"

(*WJS*, p. 337, March 24, 1844). See also *WJS*, pp. 392–93, note 5; p. 338; HC 6:272.

42. See *WJS*, pp. 340–62 for six contemporary accounts of the King Follett discourse; compare D&C 93.

43. *TPJS*, p. 361; *WJS*, p. 355.

44. *TPJS*, p. 362. The earliest printing of this discourse appears in *TS* 5 (August 15, 1844): 612–17.

45. *TPJS*, pp. 355–56.

46. *TPJS*, p. 365.

47. See HC 6:280–81, footnote; also *Contributor* 5 (April 1884): 251–60.

48. Elder Roberts commented, "The Prophet lived his life in crescendo. From small beginnings, it rose in breadth and power as he neared its close. As a teacher he reached the climax of his career in [the King Follett] discourse." (*TPJS*, p. 356, footnote.)

49. See *TPJS*, pp. 369–76, June 16, 1844.

50. *JI* 27 (August 1, 1892): 471.

51. See HC 6:551.

52. HC 6:497. George A. Smith's Journal History summary of the Prophet's remarks is based on statements of Joseph Hovey and others. See also journal of Joseph Lee Robinson, p. 22.

53. HC 6:499.

54. See journal of John Pulsipher, p. 13.

55. HC 6:499.

56. See, for instance, journal of James Palmer.

57. See the journals of Joseph Lee Robinson, p. 22; Samuel H. Rogers, p. 63; Wandle Mace, p. 134; and John Pulsipher, p. 13.

58. HC 6:499, 500.

59. See *TPJS*, p. 377; journal of Wandle Mace, p. 308.

60. *TPJS*, p. 377; HC 6:545, 549.

61. *TPJS*, p. 376; HC 6:545–46.

62. For the affidavits on mob movements and munitions, see HC 6:500–531.

63. See Vilate Kimball's letter of June 24 to her husband, Heber C. Kimball: "Some were dreadfully tried in their faith to think Joseph should

leave them in the hour of danger. Hundreds have left; the most of the merchants on the hill have gone." (As cited in Whitney, *Life of Heber C. Kimball*, p. 340.) See also journal of Wandle Mace, p. 144.

64. John Murdock, in *Southern Star* 1 (March 11, 1899): 117.

65. *TPJS*, pp. 377–78; HC 6:549–50.

66. *Southern Star* 1 (March 11, 1899): 117.

67. *JI* 27 (July 1, 1892): 400.

68. See *Writings*, p. 611; *TPJS*, p. 391; HC 6:605.

69. See testimony of Leonora Taylor in undated manuscript under "Carthage," Church Archives, The Church of Jesus Christ of Latter-day Saints, Salt Lake City, Utah.

70. See diary of George Laub, p. 32.

71. Compare an 1846 statement from the high council of the Church: "We have never tied a black strap around any person's neck, neither have we cut their bowels out, nor fed any to the 'Cat-fish' " (*TS* 6 [January 20, 1846]: 1097).

72. William Fawcett recalled a public address in which Joseph referred to the price on his head (see *JI* 27 [January 15, 1892]: 66). Only four weeks before his death he told Reynolds Cahoon and Alphaeus Cutler that he wanted his body to be buried next to his father, "if they do not get it"—meaning, if his enemies did not take his body (see journal of Anson Call). Also, Mother Smith said there was an "immense reward which was offered by the Missourians for Joseph's head" (*History of Joseph Smith*, p. 324).

73. HC 6:554.

74. See Hinckley, *Daniel H. Wells*, p. 34; also HC 6:554.

75. See recollection of Mary Ellen Kimball in *JI* 27 (August 15, 1892): 490–91.

76. HC 6:554.

77. Journal of Isaac Haight, p. 13.

78. "Autobiography of John Lowe Butler," p. 28.

79. John Bernhisel wrote that Joseph looked him full in the face when he made this statement. This occurred after armed horsemen, sixty or more, came round the bend and Joseph halted his company and said: "Do not be alarmed brethren. They can only do what they did to the an-

cient saints. They can only kill the body." They turned out to be militiamen. See Journal History, June 24, 1844.

80. HC 6:592.

81. HC 6:603.

82. See HC 6:605–6.

83. See account given by John Taylor in Appendix 4 of Roberts, *Rise and Fall*, p. 441.

84. See Stephen Markham Papers, compiled by Lucille Thorne.

85. See Stiles, *Recollections and Sketches: Early Lawyers and Public Men of Iowa.*

86. See diary of William Holmes Walker, p. 13.

87. HC 6:608.

88. When reviewing the Missouri persecutions, he said with resolve, "If I do not stand with those who will stand by me in the hour of trouble and danger, without faltering, I give you leave to shoot me" (*HC* 6:94). In 1842 he had said to three men, of whom John Taylor was one: "When my enemies take away my rights, I will bear it and keep out of the way; but if they take away your rights, I will fight for you" (*HC* 5:181; *TPJS*, p. 268). Earlier still he had said, "If I have power and am called on by the inno-cent suffering, I swear by the great God I will use that power for them and not say I can't do anything for you. I can do something and I will." (See journal of Levi Richards, p. 88.) In an 1841 sermon he said: "What greater love hath any man than that he lay down his life for his friend? Then why not fight for our friend until we die?" (*WJS*, p. 81.) In his last speech before the Legion, on June 18, he said, "While I live, I will never tamely submit to the dominion of cursed mobocracy" (*HC* 6:499). These sober commitments would have been empty rhetoric had he been passive during the lethal attack at Carthage.

89. "[William] Grover said they had killed the Smiths, and Jo struck him twice with his fist" (testimony of Joseph Brackenbury in undated manuscript under "Carthage," Church Archives). Grover appears on Sheriff Backenstos's list of those who were in the mob at Carthage (*HC* 7:143). It is said he went to Missouri for a time until his bruises healed. He had a grudging respect for Joseph as a "d--n stout man." (See Barnes, "The Martyrdom," p. 5.)

90. Of the thirty-six holes James W. Woods counted, many were around the frame of the east window. Jacob Hamblin discovered that all

the latches on the gates and doors had been bent down to allow easy access. (See Stiles, *Recollections and Sketches: Early Lawyers and Public Men of Iowa*; Little, *Jacob Hamblin*, pp. 13–14.)

91. See Willard Richards, "Two Minutes in Jail," HC 6:619–21.

92. See HC 6:600, 610.

93. JI 27 (March 15, 1892): 173.

94. Joseph tried to persuade Hyrum to leave for Cincinnati the day they crossed the Mississippi for Montrose. Later he pleaded with him to stay in Nauvoo rather than accompany him to Carthage. And on the road to Carthage he encouraged him to return to Nauvoo with other members of the city council. Each time Hyrum insisted on remaining with him. See HC 6:520; TPJS, pp. 376–77; Roberts, *Rise and Fall*, p. 291.

95. HC 6:618.

96. Joseph cried out when he first heard of the suffering exiles in Missouri: "Oh God, what shall I do in such a trial as this!" (Smith, *History of Joseph Smith*, p. 225.) See also HC 6:618. Henry Harmon claimed that Joseph came to the window twice, and the second time he came through. See martyrdom accounts of James W. Woods, Samuel O. Williams, and Henry Harmon, Church Archives, The Church of Jesus Christ of Latter-day Saints, Salt Lake City, Utah.

97. HC 6:618.

98. HC 6:621.

99. See Oaks and Hill, *Carthage Conspiracy*, p. 88; Cannon, *Life of Joseph Smith*, p. 525; also martyrdom accounts in HC 7.

100. See Cannon, *Life of Joseph Smith*, p. 525. Mother Smith described the faces of her two sons, as they lay in state in the Mansion, as "peaceful and smiling" (*History of Joseph Smith*, p. 325). Joseph Fielding wrote in his journal that their "noble appearance" was "by no means lost in death as they lay side by side" (diary of Joseph Fielding, vol. 5, p. 46).

101. See recollection of Brigham Young, unpublished discourse of July 14, 1861, Church Archives.

102. He also wrote the hymn, "The Seer," for the dedication of the Seventies' Hall in Nauvoo, the day after Christmas, 1844. See HC 7:333–35.

103. HC 6:621.

104. HC 6:519.

105. *Autobiography of Parley P. Pratt*, pp. 332–33.

106. Rage and restraint are manifest in these excerpts from a captain of a rifle company in the Nauvoo Legion: "At the word we would gladly have marched and met the mob in battle but that was not Joseph's way. . . . We were kept under arms until June 24, when the Legion was dismissed. . . . My feeling as I gazed on the lifeless bodies of those men . . . [was that] I would much rather at the head of my company [have] marched into the prairie of Illinois and fought the whole mob of the states until one party or the other became extinct, than tamely to have these great men murdered as they were. But the authorities who were left said, 'Be still and see the salvation of God.' " (Journal of Luman Andros Shurtliff, pp. 63–64.)

107. D&C 6:29–30.

108. D&C 132:49.

109. D&C 132:60.

110. D&C 136:39.

# Bibliography

## Published Sources Cited

### Books and Pamphlets

Anderson, Mary Audentia Smith, ed. *Joseph Smith III and the Restoration.* Independence, Missouri: Herald Publishing House, 1952.

Andrus, Hyrum L., and Helen Mae Andrus, eds. *They Knew The Prophet.* Salt Lake City: Bookcraft, 1974.

Arrington, Leonard J. *From Quaker to Latter-day Saint: Bishop Edwin D. Woolley.* Salt Lake City: Deseret Book Co., 1976.

Backman, Milton V., Jr. *The Heavens Resound.* Salt Lake City: Deseret Book Co., 1983.

———. *Joseph Smith's First Vision.* 2d ed., rev. Salt Lake City: Bookcraft, 1980.

Barrett, Ivan J. *Joseph Smith and the Restoration.* Provo, Utah: Brigham Young University Press, 1973.

———. *Joseph Smith, the Extraordinary.* 4th ed. Provo, Utah: Brigham Young University Press, 1964.

Bennett, Archibald F. *Saviors on Mount Zion* [Sunday School Course 15 manual]. Salt Lake City: The Church of Jesus Christ of Latter-day Saints, 1951.

Berrett, William E. *Joseph Smith, Symbol of Greatness.* Brigham Young University Speeches of the Year. Provo, 13 June 1960.

Bitton, Davis. *Guide to Mormon Diaries and Autobiographies.* Provo, Utah: Brigham Young University Press, 1977.

Brown, Francis, ed. *A Hebrew and English Lexicon of the Old Testament.* Oxford: Clarendon Press, 1979.

Burnett, Peter H. *An Old California Pioneer.* Oakland, California: Biobooks, 1946.

Bushman, John. *John Bushman: Utah-Arizona Pioneer 1843–1926.* Edited by Derryfield N. Smith. Provo, Utah: John Bushman Family Association, 1975.

Cannon, George Q. *Life of Joseph Smith the Prophet.* Salt Lake City: Deseret Book Co., 1986.

Cannon, John Q. *George Cannon the Immigrant.* Salt Lake City, 1927.

Clark, James R., ed. *Messages of the First Presidency of The Church of Jesus Christ of Latter-day Saints*. 6 vols. Salt Lake City: Bookcraft, 1965–75.

Conference Reports of The Church of Jesus Christ of Latter-day Saints. Salt Lake City: The Church of Jesus Christ of Latter-day Saints, April 1900, October 1926.

Corrill, John. *Brief History of the Church of Christ of Latter Day Saints*. St. Louis, 1839.

Cowley, Matthias F. *Wilford Woodruff: History of His Life and Labors*. Salt Lake City: Bookcraft, 1964.

*Early Scenes in Church History*. Salt Lake City: Juvenile Instructor Office, 1882.

Evans, John Henry. *Joseph Smith: An American Prophet*. New York: Macmillan, 1946.

*Foxe's Book of Martyrs*. Edited by Marie Gentert King. Old Tappan, New Jersey: Fleming H. Revell Co., 1968.

Grant, Jedediah M. *A Collection of Facts, Relative to the Course Taken by Elder Sidney Rigdon. . . .* Philadelphia: Browning, Bicking, and Guilbert, 1844.

Hinckley, Bryant S. *Daniel H. Wells*. Salt Lake City: Deseret News Press, 1942.

Jarvis, Zora Smith. *Ancestry, Biography and Family of George A. Smith*. Salt Lake City, 1962.

Jenson, Andrew. *Autobiography of Andrew Jenson*. Salt Lake City: Deseret News Press, 1938.

———. *The Historical Record*. 9 vols. Salt Lake City: Andrew Jenson, 1882–90.

———. *Latter-day Saint Biographical Encyclopedia*. 4 vols. 1901–36. Reprint. Salt Lake City: Western Epics, 1971.

Jenson, Andrew, and Edward Stevenson. *Infancy of the Church*. Salt Lake City, 1889.

*John Lathrop: Reformer, Sufferer, Pilgrim, Man of God*. Salt Lake City: Institute of Family Research, Inc., n.d.

Johnson, Benjamin F. *The Benjamin F. Johnson Letter to George S. Gibbs* [pamphlet, copied from typescript of original 1903 letter]. Dugway, Utah: Pioneer Press, 1968.

———. *My Life's Review*. Independence, Missouri: Zion's Printing and Publishing Co., 1947.

*Journal of Discourses*. 26 vols. London: Latter-day Saints' Book Depot, 1854–86.

King, Arthur Henry. *The Abundance of the Heart*. Salt Lake City: Bookcraft, 1986.

Little, James A. *Jacob Hamblin*. Salt Lake City: Bookcraft, 1969.

Littlefield, Lyman Omer. *Reminiscences of Latter-day Saints*. Logan, Utah: Utah Journal Co., 1888.

Lundwall, N. B., comp. *The Vision*. Salt Lake City: Bookcraft, n.d.

*Lydia Knight's History*. Salt Lake City: Juvenile Instructor Office, 1883.

McGavin, E. Cecil. *Nauvoo the Beautiful*. Salt Lake City: Bookcraft, 1972.

McKay, David O. *Gospel Ideals*. Salt Lake City: Improvement Era, 1953.

Madsen, Truman G. *The Highest In Us*. Salt Lake City: Bookcraft, 1979.

———. *Joseph Smith Among the Prophets* [pamphlet]. Salt Lake City: Deseret Book Co., 1966.

———, ed. *Concordance of Doctrinal Statements of Joseph Smith*. Salt Lake City: I.E.S. Publishing, 1985.

Millett, George Francis. *Ancestors and Descendants of Thomas Millett. . . .* Mesa, Arizona: George Francis Millett, 1959.

Nibley, Hugh. *The Message of the Joseph Smith Papyri: An Egyptian Endowment*. Salt Lake City: Deseret Book Co., 1975.

———. *The Myth Makers*. Salt Lake City: Bookcraft, 1961.

Oaks, Dallin H., and Marvin S. Hill. *Carthage Conspiracy: The Trial of the Accused Assassins of Joseph Smith*. Urbana: University of Illinois Press, 1979.

*Our Lineage* [manual]. Salt Lake City: Genealogical Society of Utah, 1933.

Packer, Boyd K. *The Holy Temple*. Salt Lake City: Bookcraft, 1980.

Palmer, Spencer J. *The Expanding Church*. Salt Lake City: Deseret Book Co., 1978.

———, ed. *Deity and Death*. Provo, Utah: Religious Studies Center, Brigham Young University, 1978.

Pardoe, T. Earl. *Lorin Farr, Pioneer*. Provo, Utah: Brigham Young University Press, 1953.

Parry, Edwin F., comp. *Stories About Joseph Smith the Prophet*. Salt Lake City: Deseret News Press, 1934.

Pratt, Orson. *Interesting Account of Several Remarkable Visions, and of the Late Discovery of Ancient American Records*. Edinburgh: Ballantyne and Hughes, 1840.

———. *Masterful Discourses and Writings of Orson Pratt*. Compiled by N. B. Lundwall. Salt Lake City: Bookcraft, 1962.

Pratt, Parley P. *Autobiography of Parley P. Pratt*. Edited by Parley P. Pratt, Jr. Salt Lake City: Deseret Book Co., 1938.

Quincy, Josiah. *Figures of the Past*. Boston: Roberts Bros., 1883.

Roberts, B. H. *A Comprehensive History of The Church of Jesus Christ of Latter-day Saints*. 6 vols. Salt Lake City: The Church of Jesus Christ of Latter-day Saints, 1930.

———. *The Rise and Fall of Nauvoo*. Salt Lake City: Bookcraft, 1965.

*Scraps of Biography*. Salt Lake City: Juvenile Instructor Office, 1883.

Smith, Jesse N. *Journal of Jesse Nathaniel Smith*. Salt Lake City: Deseret News Publishing Co., 1953.

Smith, Joseph. *History of The Church of Jesus Christ of Latter-day Saints*. Edited by B. H. Roberts. 7 vols. Salt Lake City: The Church of Jesus Christ of Latter-day Saints, 1932-51.

———. *The Personal Writings of Joseph Smith*. Compiled and edited by Dean C. Jessee. Salt Lake City: Deseret Book Co., 1984.

———. *Teachings of the Prophet Joseph Smith*. Compiled by Joseph Fielding Smith. Salt Lake City: Deseret Book Co., 1976.

———. *The Words of Joseph Smith*. Compiled and edited by Andrew F. Ehat and Lyndon W. Cook. Provo, Utah: Religious Studies Center, Brigham Young University, 1980.

Smith, Joseph Fielding. *Doctrines of Salvation*. Compiled by Bruce R. McConkie. 3 vols. Salt Lake City: Bookcraft, 1954-56.

Smith, Lucy Mack. *History of Joseph Smith by His Mother*. Edited by Preston Nibley. Salt Lake City: Bookcraft, 1958.

Snow, Eliza R. *Eliza R. Snow, an Immortal: Selected Writings of Eliza R. Snow*. Compiled by Nicholas G. Morgan. Salt Lake City: Nicholas G. Morgan, Sr., Foundation, 1957.

———. *Poems: Religious, Historical, and Political*. 2 vols. Salt Lake City: Latter-day Saints' Printing and Publishing Establishment, 1877.

Stevenson, Edward. *Reminiscences of Joseph, the Prophet, and the Coming Forth of the Book of Mormon*. Salt Lake City: Edward Stevenson, 1893.

Stiles, Edward H. *Recollections and Sketches: Early Lawyers and Public Men of Iowa*. Des Moines, Iowa: Homestead Publishing Co., 1916.

Taylor, John. *The Gospel Kingdom: Selections from the Writings and Discourses of John Taylor*. Selected by G. Homer Durham. Bookcraft, 1987.

Tullidge, Edward W. *The Women of Mormondom*. New York, 1877.

Walker, Rodney W., and Noel C. Stevenson, comps. *Ancestry and Descendants of John Walker*. Kaysville, Utah: The John Walker Family Organization, 1953.

Whitney, Orson F. *Life of Heber C. Kimball.* Salt Lake City: Bookcraft, 1967.

Widtsoe, John A. *Joseph Smith: Seeker After Truth, Prophet of God.* Salt Lake City: Bookcraft, 1957.

Woodruff, Wilford. *The Discourses of Wilford Woodruff.* Selected by G. Homer Durham. Salt Lake City: Bookcraft, 1946.

Young, Brigham. *Discourses of Brigham Young.* Selected by John A. Widtsoe. Salt Lake City: Deseret Book Co., 1941.

———. *Letters of Brigham Young to His Sons.* Edited by Dean C. Jessee. Salt Lake City: Deseret Book Co., 1974.

Young, Joseph. *Enoch and His City* [pamphlet]. Salt Lake City: Deseret News, 1878.

Young, S. Dilworth. *"Here Is Brigham . . ."* Salt Lake City: Bookcraft, 1964.

## Articles

Adams, Henry. "Charles Francis Adams Visits the Mormons in 1844." *Proceedings of the Massachusetts Historical Society* 68 (1952): 267–300.

Anderson, Richard L. "Circumstantial Confirmation of the First Vision Through Reminiscences." *BYU Studies* 9 (Spring 1969): 373–404.

Arrington, Leonard J., ed. "Oliver Cowdery's Kirtland, Ohio, 'Sketch Book.'" *BYU Studies* 12 (Summer 1972): 410–26.

Bennett, Archibald F. "The Ancestry of Joseph Smith." *Utah Genealogical and Historical Magazine* 20 (April 1929): 49–74.

Jessee, Dean C. "The Early Accounts of Joseph Smith's First Vision." *BYU Studies* 9 (Spring 1969): 275–94.

Lyon, T. Edgar. "How Authentic Are Mormon Historic Sites in Vermont and New York?" *BYU Studies* 9 (Spring 1969): 341–50.

Madsen, Truman G. "Guest Editor's Prologue." *BYU Studies* 9 (Spring 1969): 235–40.

McGavin, E. Cecil. "The Kirtland Temple Defiled." *Improvement Era* 43 (October 1940): 594–95.

Partridge, Scott H. "The Failure of the Kirtland Safety Society." *BYU Studies* 12 (Summer 1972): 437–54.

Porter, Larry C. "Reverend George Lane—Good 'Gifts,' Much 'Grace,' and Marked 'Usefulness.'" *BYU Studies* 9 (Spring 1969): 321–40.

Sampson, D. Paul, and Larry T. Wimmer. "The Kirtland Safety Society: The Stock Ledger Book and the Bank Failure." *BYU Studies* 12 (Summer 1972): 427–36.

Whitney, Helen Mar. "Scenes and Incidents in Nauvoo." *Woman's Exponent* 10 (October 15, 1881): 74.

Wirthlin, LeRoy S. "Joseph Smith's Boyhood Operation: An 1813 Surgical Success." *BYU Studies* 21 (Spring 1981): 131–54.

Zucker, Louis C. "Joseph Smith as a Student of Hebrew." *Dialogue: A Journal of Mormon Thought* 3 (Summer 1968): 41–55.

## Periodicals

*Brigham Young University Studies* (Provo, Utah). 1959–.

*Church News* (Salt Lake City). 1943–.

*Contributor* (Salt Lake City). 1879–96.

*The Deseret News* (Salt Lake City). 1867–.

*The Deseret News Weekly* (Salt Lake City). 1850–97.

*Dialogue: A Journal of Mormon Thought* (Salt Lake City). 1966–.

*The Improvement Era* (Salt Lake City). 1897–1970.

*Iowa Democrat* (Fairfield, Iowa). 1866–.

*The Juvenile Instructor* (Salt Lake City). 1866–1930.

*Latter Day Saints' Messenger and Advocate* (Kirtland, Ohio). 1834–37.

*The Latter-day Saints' Millennial Star* (Liverpool and London, England). 1840–1970.

*Nauvoo Expositor* (Nauvoo, Illinois). June 7, 1844.

*New Era* (Salt Lake City). 1971–.

*The Relief Society Magazine* (Salt Lake City). 1914–70.

*Salt Lake Herald* (Salt Lake City). 1870–1909.

*Southern Star* (Chattanooga, Tennessee). 1898–1900.

*Times and Seasons* (Nauvoo, Illinois). 1839–46.

*Utah Genealogical and Historical Magazine* (Salt Lake City). 1910–40.

*Woman's Exponent* (Salt Lake City). 1872–1914.

*Young Woman's Journal* (Salt Lake City). 1889–1929.

# Unpublished Sources Cited

Adams, William. Diary. Harold B. Lee Library, Special Collections, Brigham Young University, Provo, Utah (hereafter given as BYU Special Collections).

Angell, Truman O. Journal. Church Archives, The Church of Jesus Christ of Latter-day Saints, Salt Lake City, Utah (hereafter given as Church Archives).

Appleby, William I. Journal. Church Archives.

Barnes, Lorenzo. Journal. Church Archives.

Barnes, Thomas. "The Martyrdom." Church Archives.

Barrett, Elsie E. Sketch of Mary Elizabeth Rollins Lightner. Church Archives.

Butler, John Lowe. "Autobiography of John Lowe Butler." BYU Special Collections.

Call, Anson. Journal. Church Archives.

Cannon, Abraham H. Diary. Church Archives.

Clark, Mary Louisa Woolley. Autobiography. BYU Special Collections.

Clayton, William. Journal. Church Archives.

Cluff, Harvey H. Journal. Church Archives.

Coray, Howard. Autobiographical sketches. Church Archives.

Cordon, Alfred. Journal. Church Archives.

Cox, Martha Cragun. "Stories from Notebook of Martha Cox, Grandmother of Fern Cox." Church Archives.

"Early History of Provo, 1849–72." Family History Library, The Church of Jesus Christ of Latter-day Saints, Salt Lake City, Utah.

Fielding, Joseph. Diary. 5 vols. Church Archives.

Haight, Isaac. Journal. BYU Special Collections.

Hale, Jonathan H. Journal. BYU Special Collections.

Hancock, Levi Ward. Journal. BYU Special Collections.

Hancock, Mosiah Lyman. "Life Story of Mosiah Lyman Hancock." BYU Special Collections.

Hickman, Minerva Wade. "Sketch of Minerva Wade Hickman." Church Archives.

Holmes, Jonathan H. Papers. Church Archives.

Huntington, Oliver B. Diary. 2 vols. BYU Special Collections.

Hyde, Orson. Letter to John S. Fullmer, September 27, 1844. Church Archives.

James, Jane E. Manning. "Biography of Jane E. Manning James. . . ." Church Archives.

Johnson, Joel Hills. Journal. Church Archives.

Journal History of The Church of Jesus Christ of Latter-day Saints. Church Archives.

Kimball, Heber C. "Last Sermon of Heber C. Kimball." BYU Special Collections.

Laub, George. Diary. BYU Special Collections.

Lee, LaFayette C. Notebook. Church Archives.

Lightner, Mary Elizabeth Rollins. Journal. BYU Special Collections.

———. Papers. BYU Special Collections.

———. Remarks of Mary Elizabeth Rollins Lightner, April 14, 1905, at Brigham Young University. BYU Special Collections.

Lundwall, N. B. "Lundwall Microfilm Collection." BYU Special Collections.

Mace, Wandle. Journal. Church Archives.

Markham, Stephen. Papers. BYU Special Collections.

McBride, Reuben. Diary. Church Archives.

Minute book for Nauvoo Relief Society. Kept by Eliza R. Snow. Church Archives.

Nuttall, L. John. Journal. BYU Special Collections.

Palmer, James. Journal. Church Archives.

Potter, Amasa. Journal. Church Archives.

Pratt, Orson. Letter to Parley P. Pratt, 1853. Church Archives.

Pulsipher, John. Journal. BYU Special Collections.

Pulsipher, Zera. Papers. Church Archives.

Record of the Utah Stake of Zion. Church Archives.

Rich, Sarah DeArmon Pea. Autobiography. Church Archives.

Richards, Jane Snyder. "Reminiscences of Mrs. F. D. Richards." Church Archives.

Richards, Levi. Journal. Church Archives.

Robinson, Joseph Lee. Journal. Church Archives.

Rogers, Samuel H. Journal. BYU Special Collections.

Sharpe, J. M. Diary. Coe Collection of Western Americana. Beineke Library, Yale University, New Haven, Connecticut.

Shurtliff, Luman Andros. Journal. BYU Special Collections.

Smith, John Lyman. Journal. BYU Special Collections.

Smith, Joseph. Diary. 1835–36. Church Archives.

———. Journal. March 10, 1843 to July 14, 1843. Kept by Willard Richards. Church Archives.

———. Letterbook. 1829–35. Joseph Smith Collection. Church Archives.

————. Papers. Church Archives.
————. "President Joseph Smith's Journal." December 21, 1842 to March 10, 1843. Kept by Willard Richards. Church Archives.
Snow, Erastus. Journal. Church Archives.
Stevenson, Edward. Journal. Church Archives.
Stevenson, J. Grant. "The Life of Edward Stevenson. . . ." Master's thesis, Brigham Young University, 1955.
Utah Stake Historical Record. Church Archives.
Walker, Charles L. Diary. Church Archives.
————, comp. "Sayings of the Prophet Joseph." Church Archives.
Walker, William Holmes. Diary. BYU Special Collections.
Willey, Jeremiah. Autobiography. Church Archives.
Woodruff, Wilford. Journal. Church Archives.

# Truman G. Madsen Essays on Joseph Smith Teachings

"Evil and Suffering." Chap. 5 in *Eternal Man*. Salt Lake City: Deseret Book Co., 1966.
*Joseph Smith Among the Prophets* [pamphlet]. Salt Lake City: Deseret Book Co., 1966.
"Joseph Smith and the Problems of Ethics." In *Perspectives in Mormon Ethics: Personal, Social, Legal and Medical*, edited by Donald G. Hill, Jr., pp. 29–48. Salt Lake City: Publishers Press, 1983.
"Joseph Smith and the Sources of Love." In *Four Essays on Love*, pp. 9–25. Salt Lake City: Bookcraft, 1971.
"Joseph Smith and the Ways of Knowing." In *Brigham Young University Lecture Series: Seminar on the Prophet Joseph Smith, February 18, 1961*, pp. 23–58. Provo, Utah: Extension Publications, 1961.
"Joseph Smith: Prophet or Mystic?" Unpublished talk given as the annual Joseph Smith Memorial Sermon, Utah State University, 1982.
"Prayer and the Prophet Joseph." *Ensign* 6 (January 1976): 18–25.

# Index